W9-AHG-079

NO LONGER PROPERTY OF
FULLERTON PUBLIC LIBRARY

AMERICAN
WAR LIBRARY

★ The Vietnam War ★

THE HOME FRONT: AMERICANS PROTEST THE WAR

Titles in The American War Library series include:

World War II
Hitler and the Nazis
Kamikazes
Leaders and Generals
Life as a POW
Life of an American Soldier in
  Europe
Strategic Battles in Europe
Strategic Battles in the Pacific
The War at Home
Weapons of War

The Civil War
Leaders of the North and South
Life Among the Soldiers and
  Cavalry
Lincoln and the Abolition of
  Slavery

Strategic Battles
Weapons of War

The Persian Gulf War
Leaders and Generals
Life of an American Soldier
The War Against Iraq
Weapons of War

The Vietnam War
A History of U.S. Involvement
The Home Front: Americans
  Protest the War
Leaders and Generals
Life of an American Soldier
Life as a POW
Weapons of War

AMERICAN
WAR LIBRARY
★ ★ ★ ★

★ The Vietnam War ★

THE HOME FRONT: AMERICANS PROTEST THE WAR

by Stuart A. Kallen

Lucent Books, P.O. Box 289011, San Diego, CA 92198-9011

J
959.704
KAL

Library of Congress Cataloging-in-Publication Data

Kallen, Stuart A., 1955–
    The home front: Americans protest the war / by Stuart A. Kallen
        p. cm.—(American war library. Vietnam War)
    Includes bibliographical references and index.
        ISBN 1-56006-718-7 (lib. bdg. : alk. paper)
        1. Vietnamese Conflict, 1961–1975—Protest Movements—
    United States. 2. United States—Politics and government—
    1963–1969. 3. United States—Politics and government—1969–1974.
    I. Title. II. Series.
        DS559.62.U6 K35   2001
        959.704'3373—dc21   00-009562

Copyright 2001 by Lucent Books, Inc.
P.O. Box 289011, San Diego, California 92198-9011

No part of this book may be reproduced or used in any other form or by
any other means, electrical, mechanical, or otherwise, including, but not
limited to, photocopy, recording, or any information storage and re-
trieval system, without prior written permission from the publisher.

Printed in the U.S.A.

⋆ **Contents** ⋆

A Nation Forged by War

The United States, like many nations, was forged and defined by war. Despite Benjamin Franklin's opinion that "There never was a good war or a bad peace," the United States owes its very existence to the War of Independence, one to which Franklin wholeheartedly subscribed. The country forged by war in 1776 was tempered and made stronger by the Civil War in the 1860s.

The Texas Revolution, the Mexican-American War, and the Spanish-American War expanded the country's borders and gave it overseas possessions. These wars made the United States a world power, but this status came with a price, as the nation became a key but reluctant player in both World War I and World War II.

Each successive war further defined the country's role on the world stage. Following World War II, U.S. foreign policy redefined itself to focus on the role of defender, not only of the freedom of its own citizens, but also of the freedom of people everywhere. During the cold war that followed World War II until the collapse of the Soviet Union, defending the world meant fighting communism. This goal, manifested in the Korean and Vietnam conflicts, proved elusive, and soured the American public on its achievability. As the United States emerged as the world's sole superpower, American foreign policy has been guided less by national interest and more on protecting international human rights. But as involvement in Somalia and Kosovo prove, this goal has been equally elusive.

As a result, the country's view of itself changed. Bolstered by victories in World Wars I and II, Americans first relished the role of protector. But, as war followed war in a seemingly endless procession, Americans began to doubt their leaders, their motives, and themselves. The Vietnam War especially caused people to question the validity of sending its young people to die in places where they were not particularly wanted and for people who did not seem especially grateful.

While the most obvious changes brought about by America's wars have been geopolitical in nature, many other aspects of society have been touched. War often does not bring about change directly, but acts instead like the catalyst in a chemical reaction, accelerating changes already in progress.

Some of these changes have been societal. The role of women in the United States had been slowly changing, but World War II put thousands into the workforce and into uniform. They might have gone back to being housewives after the war, but equality, once experienced, would not be forgotten.

Likewise, wars have accelerated technological change. The necessity for faster airplanes and a more destructive bomb led to the development of jet planes and nuclear energy. Artificial fibers developed for parachutes in the 1940s were used in the clothing of the 1950s.

Lucent Books' American War Library covers key wars in the development of the nation. Each war is covered in several volumes, to allow for more detail, context, and to provide volumes on often neglected subjects, such as the kamikazes of World War II, or weapons used in the Civil War. As with all Lucent Books, notes, annotated bibliographies, and appendixes such as glossaries give students a launching point for further research. In addition, sidebars and archival photographs enhance the text. Together, each volume in The American War Library will aid students in understanding how America's wars have shaped and changed its politics, economics, and society.

The United States in Vietnam

When John F. Kennedy was elected president of the United States in 1960, few Americans had ever heard of the small Southeast Asian country of Vietnam. Shaped like the letter *S* and slightly larger than the state of California, Vietnam occupies the strategic strip of land between Laos and Cambodia and the South China Sea. The people of Vietnam were originally from China, the country directly to the north, but according to Edward Doyle and Samuel Lipsman in *Setting the Stage,*

> The Vietnamese were able to form and retain a national identity while settling in a diverse land. In this beautiful country, mountains and plains contrast with deep valleys, lush green fields, and flat, treeless grasslands. There are small pockets of desert in Vietnam, but about half the country is jungle, and nearly four-fifths of the land is covered with trees and tropical vegetation.[1]

Although few Americans could find Vietnam on a map, and fewer still had a detailed understanding of the country's history, the U.S. military had been involved in the destiny of that distant land since the end of World War II.

The French Colony

China ruled Vietnam from 111 B.C. to A.D. 939. Vietnam was divided along the 17th parallel into two separate countries during a civil war in the eighteenth century, and it remained that way for nearly two hundred years. (It would be divided in the same spot after World War II.) It was during the seventeenth century that the powerful countries of Europe set out to colonize the world and bring small countries like Vietnam under their governance. These countries were interested in Vietnam as a gateway to China—and the wealth of spices, silks, and other trade goods that lay north of Vietnam. The French first came to the country in 1757 in search of commercial

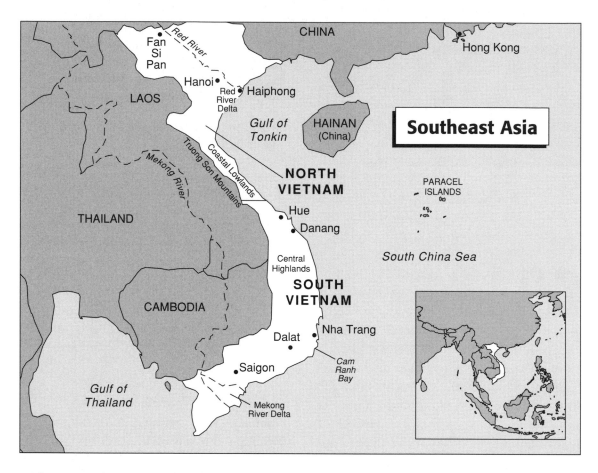

and economic gain. The first American traders arrived in 1803. By 1859 commercial ventures had been disrupted by military action as the Vietnamese capital of Saigon fell to French troops. The new French colony in southern Vietnam was named Cochin China.

The French quickly imposed their values and culture on the Vietnamese and began to exploit the inexpensive labor and abundant natural resources of the conquered people. Control over agricultural lands was taken from the majority and put into the hands of a few powerful landlords. The now-landless peasants were treated as inferiors by the French and expected to adopt French dress, language, and customs. Those Vietnamese who wanted to prosper in business and government were expected to reject their traditional Buddhist religion in favor of Catholicism.

By the 1930s, Vietnamese patriots had turned to protest and rebellion to expel the French rulers. The Communist Party led by Ho Chi Minh became the leading force of the revolution. The French responded with the first use of airpower in Vietnam, bombing Communist strongholds and arresting revolutionary leaders.

In 1945, Ho Chi Minh's Viet Minh Party seized power and, using many phrases from the American Declaration of Independence, claimed self-rule for the newly formed Democratic Republic of Vietnam (DRV) and its 40 million people. The French attempted to retake the country in 1947, and war broke out between the Viet Minh and the French, who were increasingly aided by U.S. money, military equipment, and advisers. By 1953, the United States was paying 80 percent of the cost of this war.

A Country Divided

In 1954, having lost their military base at Dien Bien Phu, the French left Vietnam. At an international conference in Geneva, Switzerland, engineered by the United States, Vietnam was divided into two separate countries: the Communist DRV in the north and the non-Communist Republic of Vietnam (RVN) in the south. The Eisenhower administration was instrumental in selecting Ngo Dinh Diem, a Roman Catholic, to govern the RVN in Saigon. Ho Chi Minh's Communist allies, China and the Soviet Union (USSR), agreed to the division. After the departure of the French, plans were made to reunify the country and hold democratic elections within two years. In addition, Laos and Cambodia were granted independence and all foreign troops were ordered to leave. Thousands of Roman Catholic Vietnamese moved to the south, while Communist supporters moved north.

The United States never signed the Geneva agreement and, fearing the spread

North Vietnamese Communist leader Ho Chi Minh (top) and Ngo Dinh Diem (bottom), president of South Vietnam.

of communism in the region, instead drew up plans to intervene in South Vietnam if the Communists should decide to invade. In the south, Diem refused to hold the promised elections, fearing that the popular Ho Chi Minh would win. Instead, Diem used his military, the Army of the Republic of Vietnam (ARVN), to destroy Communist strongholds in the south. ARVN was aided and advised by more than seven hundred Americans.

As the years passed, Diem faced growing opposition from the Buddhist majority, and brutally repressed dissent within their ranks. Promised land reforms were never instituted, and an armed resistance was organized by former soldiers of the Viet Minh who Diem called the Vietcong (Vietnamese Communists). In 1960 the Vietcong organized the National Liberation Front (NLF) of South Vietnam to overthrow Diem's government.

The NLF organized peasants within the civilian population to commit acts of guerrilla warfare. Secret supply lines from the north provided the NLF with arms to carry out terrorist acts, assassinations, and military maneuvers against government-controlled villages. With the help of sympathetic peasants, the NLF quickly infiltrated a large percentage of southern villages.

The Domino Theory

The United States became increasingly alarmed by the actions of the Vietcong. As early as 1954, the U.S. military supported the "domino theory," which stated that if one Southeast Asian country fell to communism, the rest would topple like a row of dominoes. When John F. Kennedy was elected president in 1960, he found out just how seriously the U.S. military believed in the domino theory. According to the article "Revisiting Vietnam, Again," by James William Gibson, "National Security Council policy documents from 1956 plainly stated that 'the national security of the United States would be endangered by Communist domination of mainland Southeast Asia.'"[2]

After Kennedy was elected, Diem requested more help from the United States, and another sixteen thousand advisers were sent to Vietnam. The situation continued to deteriorate, however, and in 1963 Buddhist monks, protesting Diem's repression of their religion, poured gasoline over their bodies and lit themselves on fire in the streets of Saigon. Dramatic photos of the burning monks attracted worldwide attention to the situation in Vietnam. Meanwhile, a U.S.-backed military coup on November 1, 1963, resulted in the death of Diem and the overthrow of his government. A series of coups soon destabilized South Vietnam, allowing the approximately 300,000 Vietcong guerrillas to infiltrate the south, where they used violence to induce people to support the Communist cause.

On November 22, 1963, President Kennedy was assassinated in Dallas, Texas. Vice President Lyndon Baines Johnson (LBJ) was sworn in as president and, within forty-eight hours of Kennedy's death, began

A Buddhist monk sits engulfed in flames in a protest against South Vietnamese president Diem.

making plans for military action in Vietnam. According to Clark Dougan and Samuel Lipsman in *A Nation Divided,* Johnson told Henry Cabot Lodge Jr., the ambassador to South Vietnam, "I am not going to lose Vietnam . . . I am not going to be the President who saw Southeast Asia go [Communist]."[3]

In public, however, Johnson urged caution. As Dougan and Lipsman write,

In speech after speech [Johnson] stressed the same themes: a determination not to escalate or widen the war by bombing the North or by sending "American boys . . . to do what Asian boys ought to be doing to protect themselves" in tandem with an equally firm resolve not to "yield to Communist aggression."

There was an obvious tension between those two positions, but Johnson, and with him the vast majority of Americans, ignored it. If it came to a choice between escalating the war in Vietnam or "yielding to Communist aggression," between risking American lives in a distant Asian conflict or altering the long-standing foreign policy of the United States what would the president choose?[4]

As the presidential elections approached in 1964, those questions remained unanswered. Johnson was elected by a landslide on November 3, and was inaugurated in January 1965. Members of Johnson's Democratic Party had acquired a large majority in both houses of Congress, and the U.S. economy was growing at an unprecedented rate. Most Americans were optimistic and envisioned a future filled with peace and prosperity.

Chapter 1

The First Protests: 1962–1965

Among the rights enjoyed by all Americans are the rights to exercise freedom of speech, to assemble peaceably, and to ask the government to remedy grievances. The nation's commitment to these idealistic principles, embodied in the First Amendment to the Constitution, was severely tested in the 1960s when the United States went to war without the approval of a significant percentage of the population.

This war, in far-off Vietnam, would eventually draw opposition from almost every segment of American society. In the early days, however, those who opposed the war were overwhelmingly those who were being drafted into the military to fight it. Their actions, the government's often harsh responses, and the reaction of Americans to the news on the battlefronts at home and in Southeast Asia were important elements of one of the most divisive and violent periods in American history. For almost ten years, the rights of the people who wanted to express their opposition to the war were often in conflict with the government's declared intent to wage that war.

Laying the Groundwork

Although the United States would not send soldiers to Vietnam until 1965, the groundwork for the antiwar protest movement was laid several years earlier by students who were concerned with integrating African Americans into all aspects of American public life. Although the Supreme Court had ordered schools and public facilities integrated beginning in the 1950s, in the early '60s black Americans still suffered from the effects of racism and were discriminated against in voting rights, housing, and employment, especially in the South. The struggle for equality was joined by a small percentage of white baby boomer college students, many of whom would later become involved in the antiwar movement.

Many of the first American soldiers drafted to fight in Vietnam were opposed to the war.

In June 1962, almost three years before the first American Marines landed in South Vietnam, sixty members of the Students for a Democratic Society (SDS) met in Port Huron, Michigan. The SDS was a little-known organization with big plans concerning student participation in government. The group had been supporting black students in their mission to end segregation in the South since 1960. When they met that summer on the southern shore of Lake Huron, fifty miles north of Detroit, their goal was nothing less than the basic transformation of American society.

The SDS field secretary was Tom Hayden, a journalism student at the University of Michigan who had been beaten and jailed in Mississippi after helping African Americans register to vote. When the SDS members met at Port Huron, Hayden presented a rough draft of a manifesto that would become known as the Port Huron Statement. According to Stewart Burns in *Social Movements of the 1960s,*

The Port Huron Statement was a moral critique of American society—especially of racism, militarism, and citizen apathy—a compelling vision of a regenerated society, and a sketch of a strategy for moving forward. It exalted the [ambition] for individual empowerment, for community, and for personal wholeness and authenticity; urged the translation of private troubles into legitimate political concerns; and exposed the invisible connections in the entangling web of issues that plagued the nation and the world. The heart of its message was the call for a new kind of democracy. . . . All major institutions had to be fully democratized, including economic, cultural, and educational ones.[5]

After the five-day conference ended, the organizers took the Port Huron Statement and began forming SDS chapters at college campuses across the country. Together with the Student Nonviolent Coordinating Committee (SNCC), a black civil rights group, the SDS formed a political wing that came to be called the "New Left," whose theories, tactics, and organizational tools would be used against the war in Vietnam. And these members of the New Left, according to Burns, "were well-educated daughters and sons of well-educated, upper middle-class parents, especially professionals, who politically were liberal or even further left. Relatively few were nonwhite, or from working-class or low-income families."[6]

The Gulf of Tonkin Resolution

SDS might have faded away as its enthusiastic founders graduated from college and took on the responsibilities of jobs and families. But events that took place two years after the Port Huron conference were to give the student group a focus that kept it in the public eye for almost ten more years. On August 4, 1964, President Lyndon Johnson announced on television that several days earlier, North Vietnamese ships had attacked two U.S. naval ships in Vietnam's Gulf of Tonkin.

Although he joked privately that the Vietnamese sailors were not really a threat to the navy but were "just shooting at flying fish,"[7] Johnson led the American public to believe that national security was at stake. And indeed, even as LBJ spoke, U.S. fighter jets were flying their first bombing missions over Vietnam.

Most Americans supported the president and believed Johnson when he suggested that the U.S. vessels had no

President Lyndon Johnson announces the North Vietnamese attack on two U.S. naval ships in the Gulf of Tonkin.

connection to the hostilities. They were encouraged in this belief by media coverage that often consisted of misleading statements by government officials, statements that deliberately omitted certain relevant information. For example, the public was not told in 1964 that the navy was involved in electronic espionage against the north, using high-tech equipment to perform eavesdropping, radar jamming, and communications disruptions.

Congress, too, supported the president and passed the Gulf of Tonkin Resolution, giving Johnson unrestricted power to wage a

The Gulf of Tonkin Resolution

In August 1964, President Johnson exaggerated the significance of a skirmish between North Vietnamese torpedo boats and U.S. Navy vessels in Vietnam's Gulf of Tonkin to justify the first American bombing of Vietnam. After the attacks, Congress passed a resolution allowing Johnson to "take all necessary measures" to wage war in Vietnam. The official document, the Gulf of Tonkin Resolution, is reprinted in Peter B. Levy's *America in the Sixties: Right, Left, and Center:*

> Whereas naval units of the Communist regime in [North] Vietnam, in violation of the principles of the Charter of the United Nations and of international law, have deliberately and repeatedly attacked United States naval vessels lawfully present in international waters, and have thereby created a serious threat to international peace;
>
> Whereas these attacks are part of a deliberate and systematic campaign of aggression that the Communist regime in North Vietnam has been waging against its neighbors and the nations joined with them in the collective defense of their freedom; and
>
> Whereas the United States is assisting the peoples of southeast Asia to protect their freedom and has no territorial, military or political ambitions in that area, but desires only that these peoples should be left in peace to work out their own destinies in their own way: Now, therefore, be it resolved by the Senate and House of Representatives of the United States of America in Congress assembled,

That the Congress approves and supports the determination of the President, as Commander in Chief, to take all necessary measures to repel any armed attack against the forces of the United States and to prevent further aggression.

The USS C. Turner Joy, *one of the ships involved in the 1964 Gulf of Tonkin incident.*

war in Vietnam without ever formally declaring war. According to editor Peter B. Levy,

> Although the president did not submit concrete evidence verifying the North Vietnamese attack . . . and information gathered later would cast doubt on nearly all of his assertions regarding the incident, the [Gulf of Tonkin] resolution was passed unanimously in the House of Representatives and by a 98-2 margin in the Senate. As a sign of the public's lack of concern over Vietnam, very few Americans objected to the resolution at the time.[8]

The Free Speech Movement

Levy's observation about American indifference to the Gulf of Tonkin Resolution seemed to apply to the twenty-seven thousand students at the University of California at Berkeley. But a protest movement was forming there that would be widely mimicked on campuses across the country during the following decade. The political cause that was sweeping across the Berkeley campus, stirring emotions, and radicalizing students was over a newly enacted campus policy that forbade political activities and fund-raising on campus. This ban also included activities that occurred on a small strip of nonschool, city property near the campus's main entrance on Telegraph Avenue.

The ban had been enacted because students (and some nonstudents) were using the campus to organize demonstrations against job and housing discrimination in the San Francisco and Oakland area. Jack Weinberg, a campus organizer for the Congress of Racial Equality (CORE) and the man who coined the phrase "don't trust anyone over thirty," explains the ban:

> [The] business community had been putting on pressure. They felt that the campus was being used as a base for organizing all these tactics, and that this was intolerable. We saw the movement as something beneficial to society, but they didn't, and they wanted it stopped. The university had been let to know that if they couldn't stop all this organizing on campus, their funding was going to be affected.
>
> You couldn't urge a particular issue, you couldn't raise money, you couldn't mount a demonstration, you couldn't hold a rally, you couldn't give speeches. All this was prohibited.[9]

When the ban was announced on September 21, more than two hundred students picketed. On October 1, Weinberg set up a twelve-foot-long table on Telegraph to hand out pamphlets and raise funds for CORE. At noon, Weinberg was arrested and placed in a police car. A huge crowd spontaneously gathered around the car and prevented it from leaving the scene. Students jumped on the roof of the car and began to make speeches. For the next thirty-two hours, several thousand students kept Weinberg and the police car immobilized while police negotiators tried to achieve a peaceful settlement to the protest. Burns writes,

> Through the afternoon and evening countless students waited in line to taste the forbidden fruit of free speech atop the car's sagging roof. . . . The next evening [student leader Mario] Savio announced an agreement [to resolve the issue] with the administrators . . . . [The] protesters freed the police car, later paying to repair its badly dented

roof, but the peace treaty turned out to be just a temporary truce.[10]

In those critical hours, the Berkeley Free Speech Movement (FSM) was born. Student organizations from every side of the political spectrum joined together to negotiate the rights to free speech on campus property. After Thanksgiving recess, campus

---

Mario Savio, a leader of the Free Speech Movement, speaks to the huge crowd assembled at Sproul Hall at the University of California at Berkeley in 1964.

administrators announced that seven student organizers would be expelled because they continued their political activities on campus. After this proclamation, more than one thousand students took over the administration headquarters at Sproul Hall. Mario Savio made a speech that would become part of '60s legend:

> There's a time when the operation of the machine becomes so odious, makes you so sick at heart, that you can't take part. . . . And you've got to put your bodies upon the gears and upon the wheels, upon the levers, upon all the apparatus, and you've got to make it stop. And you've got to indicate to the people who run it, to the people who own it, that unless you're free, the machine will be prevented from working at all.[11]

Governor Edmund G. Brown ordered the police to arrest the protesters, and more than eight hundred people were taken to jail for the Sproul Hall sit-in. At the time, it was the biggest mass arrest on any campus in American history. On December 8, after a strike by graduate students that shut down the campus, the administration gave in to the demands of the FSM, and political advocacy was returned to the Berkeley campus. The students had won, and with their first taste of victory, they learned lessons in organization, protest, and resistance that would soon be called into service when President Johnson ordered the first troops to Vietnam.

Revolution on Telegraph Avenue

With the help of the SDS, news of the Free Speech Movement spread to college campuses in other areas of the country. At the same time, white students who were involved in the civil rights movement began to bring marijuana from the inner cities to the college campuses for the first time. At Berkeley, this combination of drugs and protest changed the campus practically overnight. In his typically exaggerated style, Jerry Rubin, who would later found the Yippies!, explains the transition in his book *Do It!*

> The Free Speech Movement invited young kids to come to Berkeley for the action. So thousands of refugees from New York and the Midwest flocked to live on the streets of Berkeley.

> It was an easy life. The weather was warm and the seasons hardly changed. . . . You could always get by selling dope. Or you could hawk the [underground newspaper the Berkeley] *Barb* on weekends and make enough money for the rest of the week. There were always some guilty professors to panhandle. And some people started handicraft industries—sold jewelry, candles and other things they made—right on the Avenue.

> Dig the straight student who came out of a Los Angeles suburb to get an education at Berkeley. Heading for his dor-

mitory or apartment after a hard day at school, he passed down Telegraph Avenue: like walking through the revolution on the way home.[12]

In early February 1965, the Berkeley student newspaper announced that the Free Speech Movement, having won its battles, was dissolved. On February 15, however, the Vietcong attacked the U.S. Army barracks in Pleiku, killing several American soldiers. Johnson used this attack to initiate "Operation Rolling Thunder," a massive bombing against North Vietnam. On March 8, fifty thousand U.S. Marine combat ground forces landed in Da Nang, South Vietnam, ostensibly to protect the U.S. Air Force base there. By the end of the year another 150,000 Marines and army troops would be stationed in Da Nang.

The First Teach-Ins

Even with this new escalation of the war, Johnson continued to minimize the significance of America's growing involvement in Vietnam. At the same time he was escalating the war, Johnson was trying to get Congress to approve landmark domestic legislation known as the Great Society programs, which included Medicare, the War on Poverty, and the Civil Rights Act of 1965. With the American economy booming, Johnson insisted that taxes could pay for "guns and butter," assuring the public that the war in Vietnam would not be funded at the expense of his costly new social programs. A memorandum from the

Bloody Sunday in Selma

The Free Speech Movement protests at Berkeley brought college business to a standstill, but remained peaceful. A civil rights protest in Birmingham, Alabama, several months later turned into a bloody confrontation with police. Clark Dougan and Samuel Lipsman explain the situation in *A Nation Divided*:

> The Vietnam War was not the only battle heating up in the early months of 1965. On Sunday, March 7, the day before the first two combat battalions of U.S. Marines landed on the beaches of Da Nang, South Vietnam, a group of about 500 blacks gathered along U.S. Route 80 on the outskirts of Selma, Alabama. Organized by Dr. Martin Luther King, Jr. . . . they were about to embark on a fifty-mile protest march from Selma to Montgomery, the state capital, to cap off a voter registration drive that had begun two months before. Carrying satchels of provisions and bedrolls, the marchers proceeded a few hundred yards and then found their path barred by more than 150 local policemen and state troopers, 15 of them mounted on horseback. Dallas County Sheriff James G. Clark warned that they had "two minutes to turn around and go back," but the marchers stood silently and did not budge. Moments later, the phalanx of helmeted troopers moved in with tear gas, clubs, whips, and cattle prods . . . and drove the demonstrators back into the city. More than 50 were seriously injured.
>
> Coming at the end of an ugly campaign that had seen thousands of civil rights workers, including King himself, repeatedly harassed and jailed, Selma's "Bloody Sunday" triggered an uproar unprecedented in the annals of the civil rights movement. Across the nation clergymen, governors, state legislatures, and labor unions thundered denunciations. University campuses seethed.

National Security Agency (NSA) quoted in Terry H. Anderson's *The Movement and the Sixties* stated that the "President desires that . . . publicity [of the escalation of the war] be avoided by all possible precautions . . . [and the President wants to] go to war without arousing the public ire."[13]

Polls indicated that Johnson's bombing of North Vietnam was approved by about 80 percent of the American public. But

Johnson was not aware that many of the 20 percent who opposed the war were very vocal and organized, especially on college campuses. And influential college professors were starting to join their students in opposing the war. From New York to Michigan, distinguished academics joined radical graduate students to hold a series of "teach-ins" to inform students about the war. Anderson explains,

[The] campus antiwar movement first received national attention when almost fifty professors decided to hold a "teach-

In 1965, President Johnson sent U.S. bombers to attack North Vietnamese targets in retaliation for a Vietcong attack on American soldiers in Pleiku.

in" at the University of Michigan. Inspired by civil rights sit-ins and freedom schools, and just days after the Selma march, 200 professors took out an ad in the *Michigan Daily* appealing to students to join them in a teach-in in an attempt to "search for a better policy." Throughout the night of March 24–25 more than 3000 students and faculty participated in lectures, debates, and discussions. As Professor Marc Pilisuk described it, "One honors student later told me that this was her first educational experience provided by the university during four years' attendance. . . . Some who had hardly ever spoken in class before argued for an hour in the halls with white-haired full professors." The next morning 600 remained, and they held a rally in front of the library. Like those who had participated in Mississippi Summer or the Free Speech Movement at Berkeley, Michigan activists noted that participating in the teach-in changed their lives, and they remembered a night when "people who really cared talked of things that really mattered." The movement was growing, and it spread to other campuses. That spring teach-ins were held at about 35 universities. . . . Berkeley held the largest and longest teach-in; 20,000 participated for 36 hours. . . . At Oregon, the teach-in was the first sign of social activism there since the 1930s. Some 3000 jammed into the student union and listened to speakers, poets, and folk-

singers. . . . One . . . coed wore a homemade card pinned to her sweater, "Let's make love, not war."[14]

The March on Washington

The antiwar teach-ins were used as a base to organize the first large-scale anti–Vietnam War march in Washington, D.C. With coordination by the SDS, fliers were passed out at campuses across the country calling for a mass rally on April 17—Easter Sunday. SDS organizers expected around ten thousand people to attend the event, and many were surprised when over twenty thousand people showed up to protest. By noon on that sunny spring day, a huge line of demonstrators carrying picket signs completely encircled the White House. At 12:30 the crowd marched together to the Washington Monument as folksinger Phil Ochs led the group in song. Speeches were made by journalists, a senator, and rally organizers. Singer Judy Collins sang "The Times They Are A-Changin'" by emerging folk legend Bob Dylan.

Many of those gathered at the march believed that Vietnam was not only harming the Vietnamese but also leading the American government down the path to corruption. SDS President Paul Potter exclaimed,

The incredible war in Vietnam . . . has provided the razor, the terrifying sharp cutting edge that has finally severed the last vestige of illusion that morality and democracy are the guiding principles of

American foreign policy. . . . What in fact has the war done for freedom in America? It has led to even more vigorous governmental efforts to control information, manipulate the press [as with the Gulf of Tonkin incident] and pressure and persuade the public through distorted or downright dishonest documents. . . .

What kind of system . . . is it that justifies the United States or any country

Bob Dylan

Rock superstar Bob Dylan was not yet twenty-five years old in April 1965 when the first antiwar march was held in Washington, D.C. Dylan, however, had already written several songs that quickly became anthems of the peace and civil rights movements, and would soon become the soundtrack for the '60s cultural revolution. Joan Baez was a top-selling folksinger and Dylan's girlfriend at the time. In her memoir, *And a Voice to Sing With,* Baez explains the importance of Dylan's music to the antiwar movement:

> Nothing could have spoken better for our generation than "The Times They Are A-Changin.'" The civil rights movement was in full bloom, and the war which would tear this nation asunder, divide, wound, and irreparably scar millions upon millions of people was moving toward us like a mighty storm. When that war began, I, along with thousands of others, would go to battle against it. . . . Before the first official bullet was fired, [Dylan] had filled our arsenals with song: "Hard Rain," "Masters of War," "The Times They Are A-Changin'," "With God on Our Side," and finally, "Blowin' in the Wind," which endured the sixties to become everything from a fireside camp song for German Boy Scouts to Hyatt House Muzak to the best-known anthem of social conscience throughout the world. Bob Dylan's name would be so associated with the radical movements of the sixties that he, more than all the others who followed with guitars on their backs and rainbow words scribbled in their notepads, would go down forever in the history books as a leader of dissent and social change.

For many people, the songs of Bob Dylan captured the spirit of the antiwar movement.

seizing the destinies of the Vietnamese people and using them callously for its own purpose? What kind of system is it that disenfranchises [does not allow the vote to] people in the South, leaves millions upon millions of people throughout the country impoverished and excluded from the mainstream and promise of American society . . . and still persists in calling itself free and still persists in finding itself fit to police the world?[15]

After Potter's speech, the crowd marched to the U.S. Capitol, where it presented a "Petition to Congress" calling for an end to the war.

The march on Washington made national headlines, and in the following weeks some opposition to the war began to emerge in Congress. Arkansas senator J. William Fulbright, head of the Senate Foreign Relations Committee, denounced the bombing in North Vietnam, and a Gallup poll showed that 33 percent of Americans now opposed escalation of the war.

Stepping Up the Pressure

Just as the war was driving a wedge between many segments of American society, it was also dividing opinions within organizations such as the SDS, which was originally formed to assist blacks in the fight for equal rights. When the organization met in Michigan on June 9, 1965, a wide-ranging debate ensued over whether the group should focus on community-based programs or be-

come the nation's largest antiwar organization. This dilemma was explored by Thomas Powers in *The War at Home:*

SDS's inability to make up its mind on this issue left leadership of the antiwar movement open to all comers, and a variety of radical, civil rights, and peace groups attempted to fill the gap. SDS continued to be active on campuses across the country, focusing protests on the draft, military research, and the use of napalm, but it did not again sponsor a national action until its last, in October 1969.[16]

Without national direction from the SDS, a new organization was formed during a series of peace demonstrations in Washington from August 6–9, 1965, on the twentieth anniversaries of the atomic bombing of Hiroshima and Nagasaki, Japan. A group called the National Coordinating Committee to End the War in Vietnam (NCC) gathered thirty-three separate peace groups into one organization.

About one thousand people attended the peace rallies, and when they marched from the Washington Monument to the Capitol, two members of the American Nazi Party splashed the marchers with red paint. When the marchers reached a line of police, they sat down, and about 350 were arrested when they ignored orders to leave. The mass arrest made headlines, and one of the organizers, Dave Dellinger, refused to pay the $300 fine for trespassing.

Believing in the righteousness of his cause, Dellinger spent thirty days in jail, which also brought publicity to the antiwar movement.

Stopping the Troop Trains

While the SDS was engaged in high-level political debates, the antiwar movement was taking on a life of its own on the West Coast. When the bombs began to fall in Vietnam, the Berkeley Free Speech Movement was transformed almost overnight into the Vietnam Day Committee (VDC), which was formed to organize the teach-in on March 23–24. After the teach-in, Jerry Rubin—one of the founders of the VDC—continued the antiwar activism. Rubin explained the mission of the VDC:

> We were putting out a weekly newspaper, organizing door-to-door discussions about Vietnam in the black ghetto in Oakland, sending out speakers everywhere, leafletting soldiers at airports telling them to desert, advising kids how to beat the draft, and co-ordinating research, petition drives, massive and mini-demonstrations. No government official could come to the Bay Area without being haunted by a VDC reception team of psychic terrorists. . . .
>
> In one room crazies planned to rent planes and fly over the Rose Bowl dropping antiwar leaflets on the crowd. In another room crazier people planned

a direct assault on the Oakland Army Terminal.[17]

The Oakland Army Terminal was the main West Coast shipping point of draftees, fresh from basic training, who were on their way to Vietnam. The troop trains carrying those soldiers passed directly through Berkeley, five blocks from the VDC headquarters. Rubin, a former newspaper reporter who knew what would make headlines, seized the opportunity.

The VDC set up a "phone tree" in which ten people would each call another

Jerry Rubin, one of the founders of the Vietnam Day Committee, led the effort to stop trains carrying soldiers bound for Vietnam.

ten people when a troop train was spotted outside of Berkeley. In this way, one thousand people could be mobilized within an hour. The group painted picket signs and leaflets and on August 5 had a chance to try to stop their first train full of soldiers. Three hundred people stood on the tracks with signs that said "Stop the War Machine." Wrongly believing that the train would stop when the engineer saw the people on the tracks, the protesters had to dive out of the way as the train rolled through without slowing.

The next day, Rubin alerted the press to gain attention for the cause. As he said in an interview much later, "I was very aware of the media and how through the media a little thing can be blown up to be a big thing, and I knew how to get that front page story."[18]

The second day, hundreds of protesters sat down on the tracks. This time about thirty police arrived and tried to drive the activists away. Once again the train plunged ahead toward the column of protesters, as a few soldiers inside raised their fingers in a "peace" sign. The third day, the train conductors attempted to thwart the activists by traveling very early in the morning. By 6:00 A.M., however, more than a thousand demonstrators stood on the tracks. About fifty policemen surrounded the protesters in an attempt to box them in. The protesters broke free and ran down the tracks to meet the train, followed by police and television crews lugging heavy cameras. As the train roared past, several demonstrators jumped on the back and pulled the airbrake until it slowed to a halt. As the protesters whooped and cheered, the cameras rolled. The trains continued for the next several years, but on that day the news headlines showed antiwar activists stopping a train full of soldiers bound for Vietnam.

Prowar Demonstrators

The VDC's next move was a peaceful march down Telegraph Avenue to the Oakland Army Terminal. On Friday, October 15, 1965, over 15,000 people gathered at the UC Berkeley campus for the march. When the huge group of people reached the Oakland city line, they were met by Oakland riot police. Rather than battle the police, the wave of people turned and headed back to Berkeley.

The next day, eight thousand marchers reassembled in the afternoon. As they marched to the terminal, they were met by members of the Hell's Angels motorcycle group who opposed the antiwar activists. Rubin recalls what happened next:

> As we approached the line [of] Oakland cops, someone whispered "The Hell's Angels are at the line."
>
> [Poet] Allen Ginsberg, clanging cymbals and singing *Hare Krishna* on the truck that headed the march, was worried. "I hope there won't be trouble," he said. "They're probably there to fight the police."

[Instead the Angels yelled,] *"Amerika first! Amerika for Amerikans! Go back to Russia, you . . . Communists!"* A blackjacketed Angel grabbed the banner at the head of the march and ripped it in two.

Fighting broke out all over between Angels and [rally] monitors. Panic. Monitors pleaded with the crowd, "Don't run. Sit down." Club-swinging Berkeley cops moved in. One cop swung from left field and split open the head of a 300-pound 6-foot, 6-inch Angel. Blood spurted.

Another Angel jumped a cop and broke his leg.

But the Angels were outnumbered and finally captured. They were loaded one by one into paddy wagons and the peace marchers cheered the Berkeley cop with the broken leg as he was carried off in a stretcher.[19]

The protest had been thwarted for the day, but twenty thousand people marched on the terminal three weeks later and the Hell's Angels did not intervene. It was a peaceful protest with mothers pushing babies in strollers, hippies with picnic baskets,

Members of the Hell's Angels who supported the war in Vietnam attempted to thwart the antiwar demonstrations.

and professors carrying signs. The Oakland mayor praised the VDC coordinators for the group's behavior.

Meanwhile, across the country in New York City, another antiwar protest march of twenty thousand people walked down Fifth Avenue for about thirty-five blocks. They were met along the way by about one thousand hecklers who shouted insults and threw eggs, tomatoes, and cans of red paint at the marchers. The war in Vietnam had been going on for less than a year and deep divisions were quickly forming between the people of the United States.

Dealing with the Draft

Many of the young men who were antiwar activists in the early 1960s had an added incentive for opposing American policies in Vietnam: The Selective Service System was sending out an ever-increasing number of draft notices to conscript men into the army. And the military's desire to draft more men coincided with the huge number of baby boomers who had reached their eighteenth birthdays and thus were eligible for the draft. In 1964, 1.7 million men—the first wave of baby boomers who were born in 1946—reached the age of eighteen, and in April 1965 the Selective Service sent out 13,700 draft notices. In May the number of draft notices reached 15,100, and by July it had climbed to 27,400. In December more than 40,000 men were ordered to take their army physical, put their lives on hold, and join the U.S. military. As a result, according to *A Nation Divided,*

Protest mounted. In addition to the mass demonstrations staged by students and prominent peace groups, which typically targeted the draft as the most visible symbol of the government's war policy, draft card burnings, sit-ins, and picketing of local draft boards became increasingly common. Congress quickly responded by toughening the penalties for such acts, making violations of Selective Service laws punishable by a fine of up to $10,000 and five years in prison. Draft card burners in particular were promptly and severely punished, although hundreds of other anti-draft demonstrators were also arrested for offenses ranging from interference with the operation of a draft board to wearing a jacket emblazoned with the motto: "F— the Draft." In the meantime, the Justice Department undertook a nationwide investigation of the anti-draft movement based on speculation that many of the protests were incited and controlled by Communists.[20]

Although many protested against the draft, others found ways to avoid going into the army through the official system of deferments. The most popular method was to attend college, which exempted men from the draft until they had obtained their degrees or reached the age of twenty-four. Married men with families were often exempted, as were those who worked in defense industries. Other men whose moral

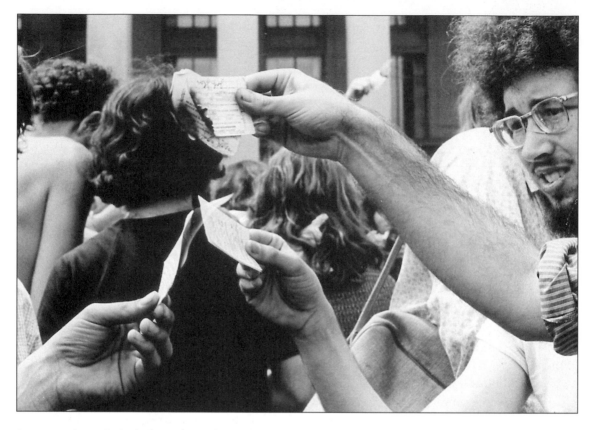

Protesters burn their draft cards on the steps of the Pentagon in Washington, D.C.

or religious beliefs prevented them from bearing arms applied for conscientious objector (CO) status.

As the war escalated, increasing numbers of men thought up various creative ways to evade the draft. Men arrived for their draft physicals dressed in wigs, makeup, and women's clothing. Some took huge amounts of illegal drugs, jabbed needles in their arms to look like heroin addicts, or even purposely injured themselves to avoid going to Vietnam. Others who failed to trick their local draft board chose to go to prison or illegally moved to Canada.

Almost one-third of all eligible draftees eventually received exemption. As a result, a significant percentage of combat troops in Vietnam came from poor or working-class families, had high school educations or less, and came from small towns. A 1968 survey of the draft stated, "Factory neighborhoods, slums (and) Negro ghettos… were the draft boards' happy hunting grounds."[21]

Chapter 2

The Escalation: 1966–1967

When Lyndon Johnson gave his State of the Union address before the U.S. Congress on January 12, 1966, he reaffirmed his belief that U.S. taxpayers could both fund such Great Society social programs as Medicare, Medicaid, and Head Start and pay for an escalating war in Vietnam.

Americans who listened to Johnson's speech that night had every reason to believe that this was possible. The American economy in 1966 was growing at a record rate. Unemployment was at 4.5 percent and consumer confidence was at an all-time high. Factories were running at 90 percent of their capacity and the inflation rate that year was a low 2 percent. These rosy economic figures, however, were about to change.

The Vietnam War had only cost the American taxpayers $100 million in 1965. By the end of 1966, however, it would cost an additional $12 billion. This money was not in the Treasury—taxes would have to

be raised and the budgets for Great Society programs would have to be slashed. Moreover, other economic problems were now causing the inflation rate to soar. As the economy slowed, prices rose, and the cost of the war skyrocketed, new groups of Americans began to question the wisdom of their president's commitment to South Vietnam. But in the early days of 1966, protest against the war was muted and the "movement" had yet to gain much notice in the realm of American public opinion.

Political Battles

By January 1966, there were more than 200,000 American soldiers in Vietnam, and several powerful members of Johnson's Democratic Party in the Senate began to express strong doubts that America could win the war. Some objected to the expense of the war; others feared that North Korea or China would soon be drawn into the war. Generals privately discussed the use of nuclear weapons against China and Vietnam,

As the cost for the Vietnam War soared, President Johnson (pictured here greeting troops) began to lose support for continuing American involvement.

and the level of fear increased within political circles. In his book *In Retrospect: The Tragedy and Lessons of Vietnam*, about high-level government decisions during the war, Johnson's secretary of defense Robert McNamara printed a memo from the Joint Chiefs of Staff:

> We cannot guarantee to maintain a non-Communist South Vietnam short of committing ourselves to whatever degree of military action would be required to defeat North Vietnam and probably Communist China militarily. Such a commitment . . . could not be confined to air and naval action but . . . [might include] the use of nuclear weapons at some point.[22]

One senator in particular, J. William Fulbright of Arkansas, was alarmed by this prospect and vehemently opposed to the war. As chairman of the Foreign Relations Committee, Fulbright held televised hearings in February 1966 questioning Johnson's policies. Fulbright's hearings gave national publicity to the issue that had been ignored by a large percentage of the American public. As Thomas Powers writes, "It was clear that a majority of the [Senate] Foreign Relations Committee was deeply disturbed by the war, doubtful of its necessity, fearful of its potentiality, uncertain what to do about it."[23] Fulbright later conducted a national tour, speaking out against the war and, to the dismay of many of his colleagues, offering words of support to antiwar protesters.

In spite of emerging political resistance, Congress continued to provide funds for Johnson's Vietnam mission. An effort by one congressman to repeal the Gulf of Tonkin Resolution was defeated by a wide margin. In addition, many Republican senators supported the war and in fact favored a substantially increased U.S. involvement.

And poll after poll showed that the war was widely supported by a majority of Americans. In fact, one Gallup poll revealed that only 1 percent of Americans said they would participate in Vietnam demonstrations, and a majority of those would demonstrate in favor of the war. Thus, opposing the war was politically difficult for Democratic congressmen running for reelection in November since this position was equated by many with appearing soft on communism.

Limited Means of Protest

In the first three months of 1966, 1,361 Americans were killed in combat—half the number that had been killed in the previous five years. The Johnson administration, however, continued its massive bombing campaign in North Vietnam.

Ironically, as the war expanded, the antiwar movement began to shrink. The year 1966 began as a slow year for the peace movement, and a year of soul searching for activists. Many members of the "Old" Left—the older generation of militants—supported working within the system to slowly derail the forces behind the war. New Left activists, however, favored more radical actions such as headline-grabbing sit-ins and strikes. A deep division over tactics completely destroyed an umbrella group called the National Coordinating Committee to End the War in Vietnam. At a meeting in Milwaukee in January 1966, the members could not agree on tactics and finally disbanded the organization. As one of its last acts, the group called for an event billed as the International Days of Protest on March 25 and 26.

Leaders of the event organized demonstrations in cities across Europe, in Australia, Japan, and the Philippines. In Rome, more than 100,000 people turned out to rally against the war. Turnout in the United States, however, was disappointing to movement organizers. The seven hundred who had come to rally in Boston were met by hostile construction workers, longshoremen, World War II veterans, and other prowar forces. In San Francisco, about thirty-five hundred people protested; in Washington, D.C., only two hundred people came to demonstrate.

New York City attracted the largest crowd, with about twenty thousand people marching in an antiwar parade down Fifth Avenue. As in earlier New York marches, the protesters endured verbal abuse, thrown eggs, and physical assault. The march represented a cross-section of America, however, with long-haired hippies, short-haired office workers, well-dressed professionals, mothers pushing baby carriages, women's organizations, and a group called Afro-Americans Against the War in Vietnam. The New York demonstration was also attended by twelve Vietnam War veterans. In the months ahead, these men would form a widely respected group called Vietnam Veterans Against the War (VVAW).

Despite these lively rallies, the total number of people who turned out to march against the war was far smaller than in the previous year. With attendance down at large demonstrations, however, some people decided to protest individually against their government's actions. Joan Baez sent a letter to the Internal Revenue Service (IRS) informing them that she would not pay her income taxes because 60 percent of the money went to the Defense Department. After Baez wrote the letter—and released a copy to the press—she was visited by an IRS agent who warned her that she could go to prison for

A mother and child lend their support to the 1966 protest in New York.

refusing to pay taxes. Instead, the IRS put a lien on Baez's house and car and confiscated the cash proceeds from her concerts, adding penalties and fines to the amount legally owed by the singer.

Baez Refuses to Pay Taxes

Joan Baez was a very popular and well-paid folksinger in 1966 when she decided to stop paying taxes that she said were paying for weapons of war. In her autobiography *And a Voice to Sing With,* Baez reprinted the letter she sent to the Internal Revenue Service to inform them of her intentions.

Dear Friends . . .

I do not believe in the weapons of war.

Weapons and wars have murdered, burned, distorted, crippled, and caused endless varieties of pain to men, women, and children for too long. Our modern weapons can reduce a man to a piece of dust in a split second, can make a woman's hair to fall out or cause her baby to be born a monster. . . .

I am not going to volunteer the 60% of my year's income tax that goes to armaments. There are two reasons for my action. One is enough. It is enough to say that no man has the right to take another man's life. Now we plan and build weapons that can take thousands of lives in a second, millions of lives in a day, billions in a week.

No one has the right to do that.

It is madness.

It is wrong.

My other reason is that modern war is impractical and stupid. We spend billions of dollars a year on [nuclear] weapons which scientists, politicians, military men, and even presidents all agree must never be used. . . . [Our] Defense System . . . continues expanding, heaping up, one horrible kill [*sic*] machine upon another until, for some reason or another, a button will be pushed and our world, or a good portion of it will be blown to pieces. That is not security. That is stupidity. . . .

Maybe the line should have been drawn when the bow and arrow were invented, maybe the gun, the cannon, maybe cause now it is all wrong, all impractical, and all stupid. So all I can do is draw my own line now. I am no longer supporting my portion of the arms-race . . .

Sincerely yours,

Joan C. Baez

Singer Joan Baez refused to pay taxes to voice her opposition to the arms buildup she called "madness."

While a wealthy performer could afford to accept the consequences of publicly, provocatively expressing her political beliefs, many average Americans found other unique ways of protesting the war. In *Who Spoke Up?* Nancy Zaroulis and Gerald Sullivan describe one such man in Minnesota:

In the spring of 1966 resistance to the draft took a new turn. Barry Bondhus, a young draft-eligible Minnesotan from the town of Big Lake, broke into his local draft board and mutilated hundreds of . . . draft records. His action was remarkable for more than the fact that it was the first of the draft board raids that would reach to near-epidemic numbers by 1969. Bondhus defiled, so to speak, the records by pouring over them two large buckets of human feces produced and collected at home by Bondhus, his eleven brothers, and a father adamantly opposed to his sons' participation in the draft. Big Lake One, as the Bondhus action came to be known, was celebrated as "the movement that started the Movement."[24]

In June, civilian protesters at Fort Hood, Texas, were joined by three army privates who said they would refuse orders to go to Vietnam. The Fort Hood Three, as they came to be known, released a letter to the press saying the war was "immoral, illegal, and unjust. . . . We have been told many times we may face a Vietnamese woman or

child and that we will have to kill them. . . . We want no part of a war of extermination. . . . We refuse to go to Vietnam!"[25] The Fort Hood Three were court-martialed and spent two years in prison.

Meanwhile, the U.S. military had decided to begin bombing petroleum, oil, and lubricant (POL) storage depots in Hanoi, the capital of North Vietnam. These POLs were in the midst of densely populated civilian neighborhoods. Many feared that in addition to violating the Geneva Convention, this act of war would widen the conflict, galvanize the North Vietnamese to fight, and incite the Chinese to join the cause. Even the president was nervous about this escalation of the war: On June 29, when the bombing began, Johnson told his daughter, "Your daddy may go down in history for having started World War Three."[26]

Protester Backlash

LBJ still enjoyed considerable support from average Americans. Those who opposed the war were often labeled traitors and Communists, and a backlash to the antiwar movement quickly developed, fueled by newspapers and magazines. Major media outlets editorialized against the antiwar activists. Anderson writes,

The press ridiculed demonstrators. *Life* called protesters "chronic showoffs" who failed to realize that the war was "a last stand for democracy or freedom or even that the destiny of the U.S. is at stake." The *Chicago Tribune* called on the

government to "act in the toughest way possible," and the *New York Daily News* demanded that the "Communist-incited beatniks, pacifists and damned idiots" be tried for treason. The *Dallas Morning News* scoffed at the "transparent motives" of the "kooks and Communists," and from Mississippi, the *Jackson Daily News* had a suggestion for demonstrators: "This is the time for police brutality if there ever was one."[27]

Police authorities were equally hostile to demonstrators. In January 1966, an SDS meeting at the University of Oklahoma was

A June 29, 1966 photo shows the results of a U.S. attack on a petroleum, oil, and lubricant storage area in Hanoi, North Vietnam.

raided by police and several members were arrested for marijuana possession. Long-haired, pot-smoking protesters were so rare in Oklahoma that the police confined the arrested men to a state mental hospital instead of prison.

Anderson describes more incidents:

Throughout 1966, most Americans supported the president and were hostile to demonstrators. In Georgia, conservative politicians refused to allow Julian Bond to take his elected seat as a state representative because he opposed the war, but that was minor compared with the situation in Greenwood, Mississippi, where self-proclaimed patriots burned down a church after a peace prayer service, or Newark, [New Jersey,] where they ransacked the SDS office, or Berkeley, where they bombed the office of the Vietnam Day Committee. Again, minor episodes compared with Rochester, [New York,] where two young men beat to death an antiwar demonstrator for expressing his views, or Richmond, [Virginia,] where an assailant murdered an activist by shooting him in the back ten times, or Detroit, where thugs invaded the [leftist] Socialist Workers Party office, pulled out shotguns, and wounded two and killed one pacifist.[28]

Religious Believers Join the Protest

By the end of 1966, there were 389,000 American soldiers in Vietnam, and 6,644 had died since the conflict began. Small protests against the war continued. On January 31, 1967, 2,000 members of a group known as Clergy and Laymen Concerned About Vietnam protested in front of the White House. In February, according to Zaroulis and Sullivan,

Twenty-five hundred members of the Women Strike for Peace "stormed" the Pentagon . . . demanding to see "the generals who send our sons to Vietnam." They carried huge photos of napalmed Vietnamese children. Pentagon guards locked the doors to the main entrance . . . so the women took off their shoes and banged on the doors with their heels. . . . Despite such unladylike behavior, unheard of in 1967 when women were supposed to be seen and not heard, Women Strike for Peace always dressed neatly and had the appearance of what, in fact, they said they were: middle-class housewives.[29]

In February 1967, Dr. Martin Luther King Jr., famous for his civil rights work, began to speak out passionately against the war. King objected to the war's violence as well as to the fact that the military was increasingly made up of poor African Americans who could not afford to escape the draft on a college campus as white, middle-class men had done. Zaroulis and Sullivan write, "The war in Vietnam was becoming a war in which black men were drafted to fight a white man's war against yellow men."[30]

King attracted large crowds to his antiwar speeches and gave the movement some respectability. He was roundly criticized, however, by the media, members of the government, and even former president Harry S. Truman.

"Hell No, We Won't Go!"

On April 15, 1967, a new group called the Spring Mobilization Committee to End the

Napalm

During the Vietnam War, the United States was using a jellied gasoline weapon made by Dow Chemical Company called napalm, and much of it was landing on civilians, causing horrible burns. When pictures of burnt Vietnamese children began to show up in magazines and on television, public opinion began to turn against the war. This was described by Nancy Zaroulis and Gerald Sullivan in *Who Spoke Up? American Protest Against the War in Vietnam 1963–1975.*

[There] had been mounting awareness of the horrors of . . . napalm B, a petroleum jelly which burns at 1000° F and sticks to whatever it splatters on, including human flesh. Dow was the only company that manufactured and supplied napalm to the Defense Department. . . . "Igniting with a roar and a pillar of red flame and oily black smoke," napalm was dropped in thin aluminum 120-gallon containers weighing eight hundred pounds, often onto Viet Cong trenches and the entrances to their protective tunnels, where it sucked out all the oxygen, leaving the occupants to suffocate if they were not burned to death. But death was thought by some to be preferable to surviving a napalm attack, since the victims, often children, were hideously scarred and crippled.

"It's a terror weapon," said one air force pilot who often dropped canisters of napalm from altitudes as low as fifty feet. "People have this thing about being burned to death."

People also had "this thing" about viewing pictures and reading accounts of grotesquely disfigured Vietnamese children. Like so many other forms of protest against the war, the protests against napalm, the public's awareness of its horrors, and the actions against The Dow Chemical Company, which manufactured it, began with Women Strike for Peace. In 1966 four San Jose WSP "housewife terrorists," "napalm ladies" were arrested and found guilty of trying to block shipments of napalm. In January 1967 *Ramparts* [magazine] ran a lengthy article, complete with color plates, on the children in Vietnam wounded by the war.

Flames and smoke fill the air during a napalm attack. The plight of napalm's civilian victims caused a public outcry in the United States.

War in Vietnam held widely attended marches in San Francisco and New York. Police estimated that the crowds in New York numbered over 100,000, although rally organizers claimed that 400,000 had attended. In San Francisco, about 50,000 turned out to protest. At both rallies, people carried banners and chanted "Hell No, We Won't Go!" and "Hey, Hey, LBJ, How Many Kids Did You Kill Today!"[31] In New York, Martin Luther King spoke in front of the United Nations building, folksinger Pete Seeger led the group in song, and seventy men burned their draft cards in Central Park.

Government agents attended the rallies as well. FBI and undercover agents from Military Intelligence photographed protesters and recorded speeches. These activities provided physical evidence linking individuals with specific events at which specific antiwar sentiments had been uttered. The courts would later rule that such spying on Americans exercising their constitutional rights to free speech was illegal.

It was never clear, however, what harm occurred or might have occurred to the thousands of noncelebrity marchers whose identities could not possibly be discovered by intelligence analysts. Indeed, some antiwar activists doubted that the government agents had film in their cameras. Rather, people believed that the true reason for publicizing the presence of photographers and sound technicians at demonstrations was to discourage the public from attending future events.

When it came to demonstrations that had already occurred, U.S. policy makers placed great emphasis on tactics aimed at persuading the enemy to ignore American protest. For example, the air force dropped 1.75 million leaflets on North Vietnam stating that the military planned to pursue the war to the fullest extent possible, regardless of the well-publicized objections that might have come to the North's attention.

Outrageous Actions

In spite of the war, the summer of 1967 was also known as the "Summer of Love." In San Francisco's Haight-Ashbury neighborhood, and in hippie neighborhoods across the country, millions of young Americans began experimenting with the psychedelic drug LSD (lysergic acid diethylamide), or acid. Starting around 1965, this drug—which was legal until October 1966—had helped fuel the antiwar movement, as people high on acid witnessed the horrors of the Vietnam War projected onto their television screens every evening. In *Sixties People,* Jane and Michael Stern describe the country's most notorious example of the acid phenomenon:

Hordes of vaguely disenchanted, vaguely antiwar and antiestablishment sixties people were encouraged by [LSD] to drop out and embark on the great grope towards a mental condition they called expanded consciousness. By early 1966, the center of the hippie universe was [the Haight-Ashbury neighborhood] where most of San Francisco's acidheads were encamped—and hundreds more were arriving every week from around the nation. They slept on the sidewalk and in doorways. They sat together playing guitars and tambourines and flutes. They sold beads and buttons and panhandled spare change and copped and sold marijuana joints and acid tabs. Hell's Angels hung out in front of Tracy's Doughnut Shop; acidheads made love in the meditation room at the back of the Psychedelic Shop.[32]

Acid and other drugs played a role in the actions of movement leaders such as Abbie Hoffman, who was emerging as a leader among the counterculture antiwar activists. In May 1967, Hoffman and eighteen others, in order to show the greed of American society, entered the New York Stock Exchange and threw handfuls of one and five dollar bills off the balcony above the trading floor. Stock trading halted as dozens of millionaire stockbrokers fell over one another to grab at the money. After they were ejected from the building, the hippies burned money on the street. That evening Hoffman's actions were featured on television news programs across the country. Although Hoffman's

attention-getting "street theater" made headlines, it alienated serious antiwar activists, who considered his actions ridiculous. And it did little to win average Americans over to the antiwar cause.

Although the stock exchange antics were not directly related to the war, Hoffman learned that outrageous actions

Music was one of the main pastimes of the young people who swarmed into Haight-Ashbury.

generate headlines. His next project was guaranteed to make the news: During an October demonstration, Hoffman told the press, he would surround the Pentagon with protesters who would chant and "levitate" the building in the air to shake out all the evil.

Active Resistance

Hoffman planned to use the Pentagon—the headquarters of the U.S. military—as the focal point of the Stop the Draft Week of Resistance organized by the National Mobilization Committee (known as the Mobe), a group of teachers, clergy, authors, and others who were calling on men to return their draft cards to the Justice Department. As usual the event's organizers were split over tactics, some wanting to hold a respectable, organized, peaceful demonstration and others, such as Jerry Rubin, urging hippies to come to Washington to "piss on the White House lawn."[33]

The week-long event began peacefully enough on October 16, 1967. In Boston, more than four thousand people attended a "mass burn-in and turn-in" rally led by religious leaders such as Dr. George H. Williams of Harvard Divinity School and the pastor of New York's Riverside Church, Reverend William Sloane Coffin. The ministers later presented a briefcase with approximately fourteen hundred draft cards to Attorney General Ramsey Clark on October 20.

In Berkeley, events began civilly that Monday, October 16, with about 1,000 people holding a sit-in at the North California Induction Center at Oakland. About 125 were arrested for civil disobedience. By dawn the next morning, however, 3,000 people had arrived at the induction center and police attacked them with tear gas and billy clubs, driving off the demonstrators by noon. For two more days, peaceful demonstrators attempted to close down the induction center.

On Friday, October 20, about ten thousand protesters swarmed into the area, some carrying shields and wearing helmets. A three-hour street battle ensued with Oakland police as protesters threw up barricades using cars, bus benches, newspaper racks, garbage cans, and potted trees to keep the police at bay. Tear gas filled the air as demonstrators blocked intersections and prevented buses full of inductees from arriving at the center. The demonstration eventually ended as night fell, but about twenty blocks of Oakland were left littered with debris and spray-painted with antiwar slogans.

Storming the Pentagon

The next day, Saturday, October 21, dawned cold and sunny in Washington. A crowd estimated to be around 100,000 arrived at the Lincoln Memorial for the usual program of speeches and protest songs. By this time, however, most antiwar leaders realized that signing petitions and protesting peacefully were not going to end the war. Mobe spokesman Dave Dellinger told the crowd that there would be confrontation,

Abbie Hoffman informs the press of his plan to surround the Pentagon with chanting protesters and levitate the building.

American flags, others waved Vietcong flags. At the Pentagon a group of radical SDS members "stormed" the building, and about twenty-five got inside. They were run down by military police, beaten with clubs, and arrested. About five thousand demonstrators surrounded the building, face-to-face with U.S. marshals armed with bayonet-tipped M-14 rifles. An additional eighteen hundred National Guard troops were on hand, along with three thousand paratroopers from Fort Bragg, North Carolina.

There was no organized leadership to keep people under any sort of control, and demonstrators threw bottles and eggs at the soldiers. Protesters who were arrested were not treated gently. According to Zaroulis and Sullivan, "Some of the arrests . . . had been violent, people being clubbed bloody. Young women had been beaten bloodier than young men, possibly to goad the men to fight to 'protect' them."[34] As protesters were beaten and arrested, Secretary of Defense Robert McNamara watched the action from his office window.

The sun went down and temperatures dropped as soldiers began to fire tear gas to disperse the crowd. Peace groups handed out blankets, sandwiches, and wet handkerchiefs to protect protesters from the

civil disobedience, and active resistance. In response to the protest, Washington was under heavy guard, with dozens of police guards surrounding the White House.

The crowd of college students, peace groups, and celebrities marched from the memorial to the Pentagon. Some carried

Protesters face a line of soldiers outside the Pentagon. About five thousand people took part in the October 21, 1967 demonstration.

gas. Thousands of people sat down in front of the main Pentagon entrance and tried to hold a teach-in with the soldiers. Others placed flowers in the barrels of their rifles.

To ward off the cold, several hundred people used their draft cards to kindle a fire, earning the record for the largest mass burning of draft cards in history. Arguments broke out between radicals who wanted to create a melee and peace advocates who wanted to simply make a point. The peace advocates won, and at midnight, as people huddled together under blankets, a chorus of voices rose up in a spontaneous version of the Christmas carol "Silent Night."

As for Abbie Hoffman, he jokingly claimed that the Pentagon did indeed rise into the air. In this bizarre passage from

America's Other War

Ironically, while 1967 is remembered for the "Summer of Love," African American neighborhoods across the country looked more like war zones. Between June and July 1967, major riots broke out in half a dozen inner-city neighborhoods in Cleveland, Detroit, Newark, and elsewhere. In the worst widespread rioting in American history, hundreds of city blocks were burned to the ground and eighty-three people were killed. Martin Luther King Jr. compared the black uprisings to the war in Vietnam in a speech at Riverside Church in New York City (reprinted in *The War at Home* by Thomas Powers).

As I have walked among the desperate, rejected and angry young men I have told them that Molotov cocktails [gasoline bombs] and rifles would not solve their problems. . . . They asked me if our own nation wasn't using massive doses of violence to solve its problems [in Vietnam], to bring about the changes it wanted. Their questions hit home, and I knew that I could never again raise my voice against the violence of the oppressed in the ghettos without having first spoken clearly to the greatest purveyor of violence in the world today—my own government. . . .

Somehow this madness must cease. We must stop now. . . . I speak for the poor of America who are paying the double price of smashed hopes at home and death and corruption in Vietnam. The great initiative in this war is ours. The initiative to stop it must be ours. . . . As we [clergymen] counsel young men concerning military service we must clarify for them our nation's role in Vietnam and challenge them with the alternative of conscientious objection. . . .

Every man of human convictions must decide on the protest that best suits his convictions, but we all must protest.

Civil rights leader Martin Luther King Jr.

Soon to Be a Major Motion Picture, he moves from a factual description of the end of a long demonstration to a solemn but utterly fantastic account of "the levitation" to rational political analysis:

Just before dawn, eleven of us assembled at the west wall [of the Pentagon]. Our bellies ached from hunger, our fingers were stiff from the frost, paint and mascara streaked down our faces. The acid had long since worn off, leaving parched throats and lips begging for Chapstick. A Shoshone medicine man asked [my wife] Anita to sit cross-legged facing the sun and lead us in prayer. Spontaneously an undulating sound arose from our circle of comrades. It was not unlike the battle cry of Algerian women. Words that shall remain secret were spoken by the shaman. Then Anita rose tall and proud, and in a voice possessed roared: OM AH HUM. OM AH HUM. OM AH HUM. The ground beneath us vibrated. The granite walls began to glow, matching the orange of the new sun, and then, before our very eyes, without a sound, the entire Pentagon rose like a flying saucer in the air.

What impressed me the most was the ease with which it happened. Child's play really. Of course, to "see" the levitation you had to be there at that moment. . . . Xuan Oanh [a North Vietnamese colonel I knew] told me he had felt the Pentagon move while walking along the Ho Chi Minh Trail on his way home.

Quite apart from the metaphysics, the sight of the most famous war-making symbol on the planet under siege by thousands of its citizens was instantaneously transmitted around the globe. That needed no interpreter, no hocus-pocus.[35]

Although the Pentagon demonstrations helped solidify the purpose of the antiwar groups, they did little to modify the government policy. In fact, just four days after the rally, American bombing in Hanoi and Haiphong was drastically increased. By the end of 1967, more than 500,000 Americans were stationed in Vietnam. During that year, 9,353 were killed and almost 100,000 wounded.

Chapter 3

The Explosive Year: 1968

In late 1967, passive resistance to the war in the form of peaceful marches and petitions was replaced by active resistance such as sit-ins, confrontations with police, burning of draft cards, and the disruption of draft induction centers. This more aggressive behavior was fueled by the demonstrations' failure to influence government policy in the direction intended. In fact, the Johnson administration was escalating the war. There was little or no dialogue between the opposing factions other than name-calling.

As 1968 dawned, many Americans braced for a divisive year. But few could predict the sheer number of tragic events that would rip apart a country already filled with protests, riots, and an ongoing war in a foreign land. As Charles Kaiser writes in *1968 in America,* the year 1968 was

the most turbulent twelve months of the postwar period and one of the most dis-

turbing intervals we have lived through since the Civil War. . . . Nineteen sixty-eight was the pivotal year of the sixties: the moment when all of a nation's impulses towards violence, idealism, diversity, and disorder peaked to produce the greatest possible hope—and the worst imaginable despair.[36]

The Tet Offensive

The first major event of 1968 was the Tet Offensive in Vietnam. The Vietnamese New Year is called Tet, and the holiday had been a traditional time for a cease-fire during the early years of the war. On the night of January 30, 1968, however, Vietcong guerrillas used the holiday lull to launch a surprise attack on almost every U.S. stronghold in South Vietnam. In Saigon, the Vietcong took over ostensibly secure areas such as the international airport, the national radio station, the presidential palace, and—incredibly—the U.S. Embassy. Within the next two days, the Vietcong attacked a total of

Views of the destruction in Saigon (above) and Khe Sanh (right) during the Tet Offensive of 1968.

thirty-five of South Vietnam's forty-four provincial capitals.

The isolated American outpost in the mountainous region of Khe Sanh near the Laotian border was hit particularly hard. Six thousand Marines were attacked by as many as fifteen thousand Vietcong. The base withstood repeated attacks for seventy-seven days. During the siege, Khe Sanh became the most heavily bombed region in the history of warfare, as more than 220 million tons of bombs were dropped from American and South Vietnamese airplanes. Anderson writes about the news images

generated during the Tet Offensive and their influence on Americans at home:

Tet produced sensational scenes, and they flashed across America in newspapers and on television: U.S. officials defending themselves, shooting out of embassy windows. Marines in Hue [near the 17th parallel] ducking for cover, firing at the enemy hiding behind scarred, ancient walls. American planes strafing villages, dropping napalm canisters that burst into rolling fireballs. A U.S. Army officer standing on the outskirts of what remained of a Mekong Delta village stating, "We had to destroy [the village], in order to save it." The haggard faces, the haunted eyes of [American] defenders at Khe Sanh. The South Vietnam national police chief walking down the street with a ragged Vietcong suspect, stopping in front of reporters, nonchalantly lifting his pistol, pointing it at the man's temple—pulling the trigger.

[Television cameras] zoomed in and showed helicopters machine-gunning peasants running below in rice paddies. "If he's running," said a helicopter crewman, "he must be a Vietcong." These scenes, these statements, became symbolic for the war. Many Americans wondered whether all the brutality would bring victory, or whether it was just pointless. Editors of *Christian Century* wrote: "This is the genius of our war effort—to destroy Vietnam in order to save it." The twisted, tragic face of war confronted American viewers, and news anchormen began to warn viewers: "The following scenes might not be suitable viewing for children." Indeed, most citizens realized in 1968 that war really was hell.[37]

The final Tet Offensive death toll was horrendous: more than 72,000 North Vietnamese, 10,000 South Vietnamese, and 5,000 U.S. soldiers killed. Hundreds of thousands more were wounded—many physically and psychologically scarred for life. In addition, more than 820,000 South Vietnamese became homeless refugees when their villages were destroyed in the fighting.

Political Bombshells

The United States managed to take back control of South Vietnam from the Vietcong after Tet. But the battle was a public relations disaster for the U.S. Army, which had been promising the American people that a victorious end to the war was in sight. CBS television news anchor Walter Cronkite, considered one of the most trusted authorities in America, traveled to Vietnam to see the war firsthand. When he returned to New York, he told his television audience,

> We have been too often disappointed by the optimism of the American leaders, both in Vietnam and Washington, to have faith any longer in the silver linings they find in the darkest clouds. . . . It seems now more certain than ever that the bloody experience of Vietnam is to end in a stalemate. . . . For every means we have to escalate, the enemy can match us, and that applies to invasion of the North, the use of nuclear weapons, or the mere commitment of one hundred or two hundred or three hundred thousand more American troops to the battle. And with each escalation, the world comes closer to the brink of cosmic disaster. . . .

It is increasingly clear to this reporter that the only rational way out will be to negotiate, not as victors, but as an honorable people who lived up to their pledge to defend democracy, and did the best they could.[38]

Cronkite's historic report on the futility of fighting in Vietnam accompanied a turnaround in public opinion about the war. Now a majority of Americans were starting to believe that victory in Vietnam was impossible.

The My Lai Massacre

During the Tet Offensive, the phrase "we had to destroy the village to save it," uttered by an army officer, encapsulated for many the futility of the war in Vietnam. But a photograph of a burning hamlet called My Lai brought the horrors of the war home to Americans in a very graphic manner. On March 16, 1968, more than three hundred unarmed Vietnamese civilians, including women, children, and old men, were slaughtered by U.S. soldiers in My Lai. An army veteran named Ronald Ridenhour had heard of the massacre and petitioned government officials and congressmen to investigate. Associated Press reporter Seymour Hersh began to investigate Ridenhour's charges, and soon stories about the My Lai massacre appeared in thirty newspapers nationwide.

My Lai was in a region of South Vietnam that had been a Vietcong stronghold for years. American soldiers of Charlie Company, led by Lieutenant William Calley Jr., were flown into the village by helicopter. Fearing that many of the civilians in the hamlet were sympathetic to the North Vietnamese, Charlie Company herded the villagers into ditches and shot them.

Military photographers recorded the carnage. Those photographs began to appear in national publications near the end of 1968 and graphically demonstrated U.S. military policies in Vietnam. As a result of intense pressure from the public, Calley was court-martialed and found guilty on March

The horrible toll the war took on Vietnam was made shockingly clear to Americans after the My Lai massacre.

29, 1971, of murdering twenty-two Vietnamese civilians. He was sentenced to life imprisonment. However, because of intense pressure from President Nixon and prowar Americans, Calley was released from prison within forty-eight hours. His conviction was overturned in 1975. Although Calley never served time for his command decisions and the actions of his men at My Lai, the photos of the dead women and children caused many Americans to question their country's mission in Vietnam.

Soldiers direct traffic in the aftermath of a riot following the assassination of Martin Luther King Jr. on April 4, 1968.

When Johnson met with his trusted war advisers on March 25, they advised the president that public support was waning and that he should halt the bombing and begin negotiations with the Vietcong—advice Johnson heeded. On March 31, the president went on television to announce the bombing cessation. Johnson then stunned the nation when he added that he would not seek a second term as president. Johnson's long, successful political career had become another casualty of the war in Vietnam.

While people were still coming to terms with Johnson's announcement, another bombshell hit the American public. On April 4, Dr. Martin Luther King Jr. was assassinated in Memphis, Tennessee. King was the most revered and respected African American leader in America and was at the center of the civil rights movement. In the week following King's death, bloody riots erupted in 125 American cities—almost every city with a large black population. Fifty-five thousand rifle-carrying U.S. Army and National Guard troops in jeeps and tanks soon rolled through the streets of America's largest cities, looking to many like the occupying army in Vietnam.

Student Rebellion at Columbia

The assassination of King created new hostilities between blacks and whites. Many blacks were becoming increasingly radicalized, some even proposing an armed overthrow of the U.S. government. Meanwhile, within the mostly white antiwar circles, many people felt that it was necessary to bring the issue of American racism to the forefront along with protests against the war. In April 1968, antiwar and antiracism politics were melded into one radical action at Columbia University.

After the Pentagon protests, according to Dougan and Lipsman, a new position paper by the SDS called for "the disruption, dislocation, and destruction of the military's access to manpower, intelligence, or resources of our universities."[39] Mark Rudd, the leader of the Columbia chapter of SDS, planned a rally to protest Columbia's membership in the Institute of Defense Analysis (IDA), an association of one dozen universities that advised the Department of Defense in matters of science, engineering, and other fields.

In the weeks after King's assassination, that rally was expanded to include a protest against racism in the United States. About four hundred SDS activists assembled on April 23 at a sundial that marks the center of the Columbia campus in northern Manhattan. They were joined by several hundred blacks who were members of the Student Afro-American Society (SAS). The protesters attempted to gain access to the Low Library, which also houses the administrative offices. When they found the doors blocked by police, the students stormed into Hamilton Hall, an auxiliary administrative building. There the protesters took acting dean Henry Coleman hostage. (Coleman was released after officials threatened to charge students with kidnapping.) Later, according to Dougan and Lipsman, "the SAS had second thoughts, not about the building takeover, but about their white allies. Arguing that black students would lead the protest . . . the blacks ordered the whites out of Hamilton Hall."[40]

By now the Low Library was unguarded and the white students stormed the building, taking over the office of Columbia president Grayson Kirk. Within the next forty-eight hours, three more campus buildings were seized by more than seven hundred students.

Students negotiated with Kirk for days, demanding Columbia's removal from the IDA. They also wanted amnesty for themselves—the assurance that no demonstrator would be expelled, suspended, or punished in any way. Kirk refused to grant either demand, and after six and a half days, New York City police were called in at 2:30 in the morning to evict the protesters. Kaiser describes the outcome:

Policemen who might have dreamed of sending their sons to such a prestigious place [as Columbia University] waded into crowds of privileged Ivy League students . . . for nearly three hours. Long-

Presidential Politics

When president Lyndon Johnson chose not to seek a second term, the field for Democratic presidential contenders was open to many well-known candidates. Johnson's vice president, Hubert H. Humphrey Jr., was the obvious choice for many Democratic supporters. Humphrey, however, supported Johnson's policies in Vietnam. Many antiwar Democrats hoped to nominate a candidate who would end the war as soon as possible.

Even before Johnson decided not to run, there was a "dump Johnson" movement among antiwar Democrats. In the weeks before Johnson's announcement not to run, Minnesota senator Eugene McCarthy came close to beating the incumbent president in the New Hampshire primary. McCarthy was helped by thousands of students who cut their hair and wore conservative clothes to come "clean for Gene" and help give the "peace candidate" respectability. During the New Hampshire primary on March 12, McCarthy lost to Johnson by only 230 votes out of 60,000 cast.

When Johnson dropped out of the race in April, New York senator Robert F. Kennedy, brother of slain president John F. Kennedy, decided to run. Charismatic and passionately committed to peace and justice, Kennedy seemed like a sure winner in the November 1968 election. Kennedy was an outspoken critic of Johnson's policies in Vietnam and promised to find a peaceful solution to the war. Kennedy easily won the California primary on June 4, but he was fatally shot at the victory celebration, two months to the day after the assassination of Martin Luther King. With Kennedy gone, the Democrats split between the prowar Humphrey and the antiwar McCarthy. They would lose in November to Republican Richard M. Nixon.

Robert F. Kennedy was a strong contender for the presidency when he was assassinated in 1968.

haired students taunted helmeted policemen with verbal abuse and sometimes threw rocks, bottles, and chairs; they themselves were subdued with kicks, punches, and billy clubs. Many students were clearly eager for a fight, but the police were far more experienced with violence than they were, and it showed. . . . Some of the students inside Avery and Mathematics halls were dragged facedown over marble steps leading to police vans waiting on Amsterdam Avenue. In other parts of the campus, away from the occupied buildings, platoons of police assaulted students wherever they found them. Outside the college gates on Broadway, mounted policemen . . . charged anyone who looked as if he might be a demonstrator. . . .

"There was great violence"; that was the understated conclusion of the fact-finding commission chaired by [Harvard law professor] Archibald Cox. . . . The Cox Commission said the administration had refused to acknowledge the fact that by the end of a week of protests, the sit-ins involved "a significant portion of the student body who had become disenchanted with the operation of their university." In all, there were 722 arrests, including 524 students taken from the buildings. One hundred forty-eight people were injured; among them were twenty policemen. A spokesman for the New York City police depart-

ment explained the behavior of his men: For the first time ever, they were faced "with the rejection of society by people who were brought up to inherit that society; nothing in any policeman's experience had prepared him for that."[41]

The Spring Marches

Though the actions at Columbia generated the most headlines, another noteworthy event occurred on April 26: The Student Mobilization Committee had called for a general strike in which students were asked to stay away from school to protest the war. Without any violence or bloodshed, over 1 million high school and college students boycotted school for that one day. It was the largest student walkout in American history. And the boycott became an international event; student strikes were also held in Mexico City, Paris, Tokyo, and Prague.

The next day in New York City, 100,000 antiwar protesters marched down Fifth Avenue to Central Park. They heard speeches by New York mayor John Lindsay, African American comedian and activist Dick Gregory, and Coretta Scott King, widow of Martin Luther King Jr. Folk musicians Pete Seeger and Arlo Guthrie entertained the crowd. Meanwhile, twenty-five hundred prowar demonstrators marched in the Loyalty Day Parade only several blocks away.

The same day in Chicago more than twelve thousand people marched from Grant Park to the Civic Center. There they were met by hostile police who set upon the demonstrators with billy clubs and tear gas. According to Zaroulis and Sullivan,

A citizens report on the April 27 demonstration in Chicago . . . accused the police of "brutalizing demonstrators without provocation." But the investigators did not blame the police entirely: [Chicago] Mayor Richard J. Daley [father of the future mayor Richard M. Daley] . . . had made it plain to the police that "these people have no right to demonstrate or express their views."[42]

The Chicago Convention

The brutality of the Chicago police was documented in a report released in August, only days before the Democrats were slated to hold their presidential convention in Chicago. Many protesters had seen the violence, read the report, and were now bracing themselves for the worst when they descended on Chicago for the Democratic presidential convention.

Democrats were in the majority in almost all political offices in the United States in 1968. They held a majority in Congress and the Senate and had held the White House since 1961. While the Republicans had nominated Richard M. Nixon during the first week of August at their

While many cities in 1968 saw antiwar protests, such as this one in New York (above), the Republican National Convention in Miami, where Richard Nixon received the presidential nomination (right), proceeded without any demonstrations.

convention in Miami without any antiwar protesters, the Democratic convention was shaping up to become a major battleground between pro- and antiwar candidates—and a violent encounter between police and protesters.

Anderson describes the hopes and fears of the antiwar movement before the August 26 convention:

> [Antiwar Democrats] feared a campaign between [Democrat Hubert] Humphrey and Nixon, one that would fail to address the issues of war and race and result in a continuation of politics as usual. Some were below the voting age—21 at that time—as were many "McCarthy kids.". . . Many drove Volkswagens, one of the only fuel-efficient cars at that time, and many had bumper stickers with the peace symbol or Peace Now! These Democrats were willing to buck their party for many reasons. . . .

> Before the convention there was talk of 50,000, maybe 100,000 activists coming to the Windy City. Journalists reported that there would be all types—hippies and housewives, students and workers, slum dwellers and suburbanites, middle-class activists with peace buttons and scraggly revolutionaries carrying Vietcong flags, and of course, old and young. "The young have never before been so much involved in politics," penned a reporter in the *Washington Post,* "have never before invested so much hope in the political process." Women [Strike] for Peace rented buses, and the National Mobilization Committee to End the War, the Mobe, announced a massive demonstration. There even was a rumor that the movement had mobilized a thousand women who would shed their brassieres in a march of the "Bare Breasts for Peace Brigade."[43]

As the convention began, activists were disappointed by the turnout. Fearing a tough police response, thousands of demonstrators stayed away from Chicago that August. Only about ten thousand arrived to air their views in the streets. City officials took a hard line against the protesters, refusing to grant parade permits or other legal sanctions.

The Yippies! Are Coming

Meanwhile, outrageous activists Jerry Rubin, Abbie and Anita Hoffman, and author Paul Krassner had formed a new organization to demonstrate in Chicago—a guerrilla-theater group called the Youth International Party, or Yippies!. Rubin writes about the founding of the Yippies! on New Year's Eve 1967:

> It's a *youth* revolution.
> *Gimme a "Y."*
> It's an *international* revolution.
> *Gimme an "I."*
> It's people trying to have meaning, fun, ecstasy in their lives—a *party*.

Gimme a "P."

Whattaya got?

Youth International Party.

Paul Krassner jumped to his feet and shouted: "YIP-pie! We're yippies."

A movement was born.

All of us in the room that New Year's Eve knew, when we heard it, that in a few months "yippie" would become a household word.[44]

The media and marketing instincts of Rubin were once again correct. By spreading the word in antiwar "underground" newspapers, *Yippie!* quickly became a national buzzword. Within one month, *Newsweek* headlines blared "The Yippies are Coming!"[45] to Chicago.

The Yippies! planned an event during the convention called the Festival of Life. Hoffman documents their outrageous plans for the week:

Crack YIP organizers throughout the counterculture held meetings for our planned Festival of Life. Events all around us were giving credence to our capsule scenario: the Democrats would gather in Chicago for a convention of death; in juxtaposition, we would gather to celebrate life. We would run a pig [named Pigasus] for president and our campaign pledge would be, "They nominate a president and he eats the people. We nominate a president and the people eat him."

We would secure a large park, sponsor workshops, exhibits, demonstrations and rock concerts in contrast to the deadly doldrums that would go on inside Convention Hall. True, there would be . . . highjinks, but our strategy did not include plans for organized violence or riot although our fanciful literature carried our dope-induced hallucinations. We revealed that the Potheads' Benevolent Association had been busy all spring strewing [marijuana] seeds in the vacant lots of Chicago, anticipating the ideal growing weather of the predicted Long Hot Summer. We spread the rumor that battalions of super-potent yippie males were getting in shape to seduce female convention-goers and that yippie agents were posing as hookers. There was no end to our nefarious plans. We would dress up people like Viet Cong and send them into the streets to shake hands like ordinary American politicians. We would paint cars taxi-yellow, pick up delegates and drop them in Wisconsin. . . .

We promised the Vikings would land once more on the shores of Lake Michigan, only this time in yellow submarines. America would be rediscovered![46]

Eleven Thousand Police

Although Hoffman and Rubin approached the protests with biting sarcastic humor, authorities were not laughing. Rumors abounded in the press that the Yippies! were planning to assassinate Chicago mayor Richard J. Daley, dump LSD in the Chicago water supply, and take over the control tower at O'Hare International Airport. Although few believed that the activists were capable of such activities, according to *A Nation Divided,* "only two kinds of people could take Jerry Rubin seriously, the police and television reporters."[47]

In spite of the hoopla, hundreds of peace organizations holding a broad range of political beliefs attempted to hold legal protests in Chicago. Dozens of meetings with city officials for permits proved to be unsuccessful. Parade permits for a march were denied, the use of a local stadium for a rally was nixed, and permits to demonstrate or camp in the city's parks were impossible to obtain. One protest leader wrote that the authori-

Yippie demonstrators at the 1968 Festival of Life in Chicago hold up the pig they nominated for president.

ties, "seemed determined to have a confrontation that can only produce violence and bloodshed."[48]

In his autobiography *Reunion,* former SDS leader Tom Hayden describes the anti-protest forces assembled by city, state, and federal authorities:

In their camp were eleven thousand Chicago police on full alert; six thousand National Guardsmen with M-1 rifles, shotguns, and gas canisters; seventy-five hundred U.S. Army troops; one thousand federal agents from the FBI, CIA, and army and navy intelligence services (one of every six demonstrators was an undercover agent, they would claim later). Electronic surveillance [wiretapping, eavesdropping, etc.] was conducted against the [National] Mobilization [Committee], the Yippies, McCarthy headquarters, and the broadcast media. The amphitheater was secured with a two-thousand-foot barbed wire fence, roadblocks in every direction, a ban on low-flying aircraft, and electronic equipment to certify the identity of delegates. The convention police command was centralized in a secure headquarters at the amphitheater, complete with giant electronic maps of Chicago, video and radio links to every security unit, and hot lines to the White House and Pentagon.

On our side were approximately a thousand people, mainly in their early twenties, waiting nervously in a park, looking for places to sleep.[49]

Battles Inside and Out

On August 25, the night before the convention, authorities tried to clear about three thousand protesters from Grant Park at the imposed 11:00 P.M. curfew. When about one thousand refused to leave, police began clubbing everyone in sight. Many of those injured were news reporters and camera operators. They had been singled out not only to prevent documentation of the harsh measures but also in the hope of intimidating journalists into refusing to cover future events. Edwin Diamond, an editor of *Newsweek,* watched the police beating members of the news media and wrote,

It became clear that cameramen were to be prime targets along with demonstrators: the police planned repression and they planned to keep it from wide public view by clubbing photographers, smashing cameras and confiscating film.[50]

In all, the police beat more than twenty-five reporters and camera operators, including the employees of all three major networks, and staff from *Newsweek, Life,* and various newspapers. Journalist Nicholas von Hoffman recorded the scene: "Shrieks and screams all over the wooded encampment area. . . . Next, the cops burst out of the woods in selective pursuit of

news photographers. Pictures are unanswerable evidence in court. They'd taken off their badges, their name plates, even the unit patches on their shoulders to become a mob of identical, unidentifiable, club swingers."[51] The police moved beyond the park, grabbing and beating innocent bystanders and couples on their way out to dinner or a show.

The next day, the action on the floor of the Democratic convention was beginning to resemble the chaos outside. Pro- and antiwar forces argued over how the Democrats would address the Vietnam War in the formal declaration of the party princi-

When confrontations between protesters and police erupted into violence, sometimes even people not involved in the protests were injured.

ples known as the platform. In the end, the prowar, or hawk, forces prevailed, defeating a proposition that called for withdrawal from Vietnam.

As politicians bickered bitterly, 90 million Americans turned on their television sets to watch the convention. What they saw was liberals and conservatives screaming at each other, black delegates arguing with whites, and, incredibly, fistfights on the convention floor. When CBS reporter Dan

Rather arrived on the scene to observe a fight, he was knocked down and beaten by a policeman, prompting Walter Cronkite to lose his famous even-handed demeanor and call the police "thugs." Anderson writes,

The confusion and madness continued for three more days, all of it sending a signal into American households—the Democrats were out of control. The party became a mirror of the nation, cracking over the issues of race and war.[52]

The Whole World Is Watching!

Things were no better on the streets of Chicago. Few protesters cared about what was happening in the convention hall— they expected Humphrey to be nominated and, if elected, to continue the war.

On August 28, the last night of the convention, approximately five thousand protesters assembled in Grant Park. As night fell, the crowd moved down Michigan Avenue to the amphitheater where Humphrey would be officially nominated. When they got near the convention center, their progress was halted by police lines. Those at the back began to push, and those in the front sat down in the streets. Peaceful arrests ensued, but at around 8:00 P.M., someone threw something at one of the officers. This set off a melee, described by Anderson:

Boom! The police exploded into the crowd. Shouts, confusion, panic. Gas canisters exploding. Police clubbing. People screaming, bleeding. Some ran down streets, into hotel lobbies, back to the park. More cops arrived. Patrol wagons appeared. Tear gas floated into the Hilton, up the air vents, and into the suite of the vice president, who was preparing his acceptance speech. On the streets, chanting. . . . "The Whole World is Watching."[53]

Police beat protesters, news reporters, and doctors and nurses who attempted to help the wounded. Inexplicably, the police charged a group of middle-aged delegates and pushed them through the plate-glass windows of the hotel restaurant.

As Hubert Humphrey was accepting the presidential nomination, television cameras cut away from his speech to show the chaos in the streets of Chicago.

After Humphrey's speech, police went after McCarthy delegates, many of them young antiwar activists who were staying on the fifteenth floor of the Hilton. On the grounds that objects were being thrown out of the hotel windows, they decided to attack the McCarthy supporters. According to Kaiser, "Using passkeys provided by the management, the police started pulling campaign workers out of their beds at 5 A.M. and beating them at random. While they were being gathered by police in the lobby downstairs . . . McCarthy . . . came down [to free his delegates.]"[54]

Thus the Democratic National Convention had been a fiasco, virtually ensuring that the Democrats would lose in November. And the protests did little to sway the American public against the war. In fact, a University of Michigan poll taken after the convention showed very little support for the protesters: Only 19 percent of Americans said the Chicago police used too much force. Another 57 percent said they used the right amount of force, and 24 percent said they should have used more force.

In spite of the public support, Johnson appointed lawyer Daniel Walker to convene a group called the National Commission of the Causes and Prevention of Violence to examine the event. Hayden writes,

> The National Commission of the Causes and Prevention of Violence . . . con-

cluded that a "police riot" was to blame for the disaster. In his introduction to the report, *Los Angeles Times* reporter Robert J. Donovan described the Chicago police behavior as nothing less than a "prescription for fascism."[55]

There was plenty of blame to go around for those on both sides of the Chicago bloodbath. And despite the Democratic debacle, Republican Richard M. Nixon won the presidential election in November by only the narrowest of margins, garnering 43.4 percent of the vote to Humphrey's 42.7. Nixon ran on a platform that promised a return to law and order and a "secret plan for Vietnam peace."[56] In spite of Nixon's "secret plan," the war would continue for four more years.

Chapter 4

Days of Rage: 1969–1970

When Richard Nixon was elected president for the first time, he vowed to unite the American people. But Nixon's victory was a bitter defeat for those on the left who had referred to the new president for years as "Tricky Dicky" because of his perceived penchant for promising one thing and doing another. Author Richard Stacewicz explains this sentiment: "Nixon campaigned on a promise to end the war quickly. When he took office, however, Nixon continued to follow the policies of the previous administration; he too concealed his plans in Vietnam from the public and used both rhetoric and intimidation against his opponents."[57]

For his part, Nixon proceeded with a plan known as "Vietnamization," which involved withdrawing ground forces while stepping up the use of airpower. And on March 18, 1969, Nixon expanded the war, by secretly bombing Communist base camps in the neighboring country of Cambodia.

Meanwhile, public opinion continued to turn against the Vietnam War. By 1969 polls showed that 55 percent of Americans opposed the war while only 33 percent supported it; the remaining 12 percent were undecided. The number of opponents had been steadily increasing and had jumped nearly 20 percent since the end of 1967.

The People's Park

After the bloodbath in Chicago, many students became even more radical on matters of war and race. In the single month of February 1969, students trashed nine buildings at the University of Wisconsin in Madison; stink bombs were set off in six buildings at the University of Chicago; five hundred students occupied a building at American University in Washington, D.C.; and major disturbances were reported at several other campuses from Texas to Indiana.

The longest and most violent protests occurred at the University of California at Berkeley. According to Hayden,

The Draft Lottery

When Nixon became president in 1969, he changed the way men were drafted into the army in order to defuse some of the protests against the war. Before, all men ages nineteen to twenty-six were eligible for the draft, but Nixon instituted a lottery system that picked draftees by their birthdays. Elaine Woo explains in an April 22, 2000, story in the *Los Angeles Times:*

> On the evening of Dec. 1, 1969, a New York congressman . . . stood beside a glass bowl in a tiny Washington, D.C., auditorium. Just after 8 p.m., he got the signal to plunge his hand into a cylindrical bowl, which was filled with 366 blue plastic capsules. Each one contained a slip of paper inscribed with a birth date. . . .
>
> The event was the nation's first military draft lottery since World War II, one of four that would be held from 1969 to 1973. The targets were 850,000 American men ages 19 to 26—men who had not yet served in America's longest and most hated war. . . .
>
> Having one of the first 100 or so birth dates meant that you'd better start packing your bags for Vietnam. Or Canada [to escape the draft]. . . .
>
> By using randomly chosen birthdays to determine the order of the draft selection, the lottery... was intended to level the playing field, putting all eligible men at equal risk of mandatory military duty. . . .
>
> The lottery also served a political end: Hoping to quell the shouts across campus of "Hell, no, we won't go," Nixon saw the new system as a way to deflate the antiwar movement. It was a canny move.

The first draft lottery capsule is drawn on December 1, 1969.

From fall 1968 through spring 1969 in Berkeley, there were six major confrontations involving twenty-two days of fighting in the streets; over two thousand arrests; 150 suspensions or expulsions from the University; forty days of occupation by police forces from surrounding cities; twenty-two days of National Guard occupation; four months of locally declared state-of-disaster conditions and five months of "extreme emergency" declared by [then-governor Ronald] Reagan.[58]

Most of these confrontations were over the war and other issues, but the bloodiest episode took place in May when students took over a small off-campus vacant lot that belonged to the university. According to Hayden, the open space was used as a "hangout" for "legions of hippies, teenage runaways, sidewalk jewelers, and tarot [card] readers, not to mention revolutionary leafleteers who dominated the once-respectable south-campus area."[59]

Before long, the hippies and students cleaned up the lot, planted grass, installed benches, built swings for children, and dubbed the area the "People's Park." The university would not tolerate the "liberation" of its land by a group of activists, and Berkeley police moved in at 5:00 A.M. on May 15, 1969, to build an eight-foot-high chain-link fence around the disputed land. By afternoon, more than five thousand people had assembled at Sproul Plaza to protest the move by the university. The crowd marched three blocks to the park, where they were met by police in full riot gear. Thus began a record-setting seventeen days of street fighting that ended when thirty thousand people assembled to protest at the park.

The final confrontation was also historic for another reason. According to Hayden, "During those days, scenes of the Vietnam War were replayed on college campuses for the first time. The Alameda County sheriffs carried shotguns loaded, not only with [less lethal] birdshot but with deadly double-O [ought] buckshot, never before used against students. [During the course of the demonstration, about] 150 demonstrators were shot and wounded, many in the back."[60] Several of these students were permanently disabled, a few blinded by the buckshot. One student was killed.

On May 16, students who came to save People's Park were violently forced into Sproul Plaza by club-wielding National Guard troops in gas masks. No one was allowed to leave the plaza, and many of those gathered were simply students on their way to or from class. Under the authority of Governor Reagan, National Guard helicopters flew over the trapped students and dropped canisters of tear gas on the crowd. The result was thousands of vomiting, coughing, and crying students with no access to water or bathrooms. Reagan's answer to those who criticized this move was, "If the students want a bloodbath, let's get it over with."[61]

The university eventually reclaimed the "People's Park," but students soon took over another lot nearby and built another park.

National Guardsmen clear downtown Berkeley of protesters during the People's Park incident in May 1969.

The Chicago Seven

The battles in Berkeley were closely watched by authorities in Washington, such as Assistant Attorney General Richard Kleindienst, who said, "We're going to enforce the law against draft-evaders, against radical students, against deserters, against civil disorders. . . . If we find that any of these radicals, revolutionary, anarchistic kids violate the law, we'll prosecute."[62]

To prove the point, Nixon's Justice Department handed down indictments against David Dellinger, Tom Hayden, Abbie Hoff-man, Jerry Rubin, Bobby Seale (a leader of the Black Panther Party), and three others for conspiracy to incite a riot during the Democratic convention. Members of the group were known as the Chicago Seven (one of the original eight defendants was dropped from the case before the trial began). They belonged to the SDS, the Yippies!, the Black Panthers, and the Mobe. According to reporter Seymour Hersh, Nixon's strategy in pursuing the Chicago Seven was to "weaken the anti-war movement, and . . . to isolate the anti-war activists

Woodstock

One of the most violent years in student protest is also remembered for three days of "peace, love, and music" at the Woodstock Music and Art Festival held in Bethel, New York, in August 1969. Although few still talk about the student takeover of Columbia University in April, 1968, the Woodstock festival has gone down in history as the defining moment of the '60s, and a "metaphor for a generation," according to the book *A Nation Divided*.

A half million young people crowded into a field on the weekend of August 15, creating the third largest city in New York. They survived terrible rainstorms, overflowing toilets, shortages of food and water, and massive traffic jams. They were rewarded with a peaceful "love-in" atmosphere, and with stunning performances by the Who, Jefferson Airplane, Janis Joplin, Arlo Guthrie, Richie Havens, Santana, and others. After the festival was nearly over, Jimi Hendrix blasted the "Star Spangled Banner" from his Stratocaster guitar, and the shrieking feedback of the national anthem became an instant anthem of the antiwar movement. Frightening, haunting, and beautiful, it was an homage to the soldiers fighting the war and a distress call for a nation torn apart by the war.

Jimi Hendrix, one of the performers at the Woodstock festival of 1969.

who . . . had yet to take to the streets in protest."[63] FBI chief J. Edgar Hoover added, "A successful prosecution of this type would be a unique achievement of the [FBI] and should seriously disrupt and curtail the activities of the New Left."[64]

Whatever Nixon's plans, the trial that began on September 23, 1969, in Chicago quickly turned into a circus. The ringleaders were Abbie Hoffman and Jerry Rubin, who appeared in court dressed in judicial robes, shirts like those worn by Chicago police, and other outlandish costumes.

At the trial, the government attempted to prove that the Chicago riots were a carefully planned conspiracy by a few radicals. The defense countered that it was a spontaneous demonstration by large numbers of people who wanted to end the war. The defense, according to Hoffman, "ran the panorama of movement activity. . . . We presented testimony from singers: Phil Ochs . . . Judy Collins, Arlo Guthrie, Pete Seeger. . . . We brought in poets, playwrights, comedians, eyewitnesses, even a member of the British Parliament."[65]

Bobby Seale, the only African American in the group, shouted continually that he was being unfairly tried and called the seventy-four-year-old judge a racist. In response, the judge ordered Seale shackled in chains and gagged. Anderson writes, "It was the first time in years an American had been gagged in court, and to many activists it was fitting: a black man in a white man's court chained to his chair for shouting his views."[66]

Six of the seven men were finally found guilty, and also handed long prison sentences for contempt of court charges they had accumulated while disrupting the proceedings. (Dellinger, for instance, had thirty-two contempt charges that earned him two years, five months, and sixteen days in jail.) When the verdicts were announced, riots and demonstrations broke out all over the country. Rubin told the judge that by convicting him, "you radicalized more young people than we ever could. You're the country's top Yippie!"[67]

On February 28, 1970, the Chicago defendants were released from prison pending appeals. On November 1, 1972, the U.S. Court of Appeals reversed the convictions, citing "numerous judicial errors"[68] in the conduct of the trial.

Vietnam Moratorium Day

Influential members of the government claimed that the Chicago Seven defendants

Chicago Seven members (top row, left to right, Jerry Rubin, Abbie Hoffman, and Tom Hayden), Bobby Seale (lower left), David Dellinger (lower right), and three others.

were leaders of the antiwar movement and that the movement would slow down or stop with them in jail. This was proven false when a massive demonstration took place while the trial was in progress. October 15, 1969, was declared Vietnam Moratorium Day. (A moratorium is the suspension of an ongoing activity. In this case, people who opposed the war were expected to express this publicly by not going to work.)

Rather than seeking violent confrontations, the event organizers spent months lining up endorsements of nonradical politicians and business leaders. Before the event, senators, congressmen, union leaders, and even a former Supreme Court justice gave their support to the moratorium.

In stark contrast to the upheavals of earlier protests, Vietnam Moratorium Day was observed peacefully by millions of people across America. Zaroulis and Sullivan recount the event:

> Only a few minor incidents of violence were reported, and these, as often as not, involved the presence of anti-demonstration hecklers. There were no ugly mob scenes; instead, in town after town, there were silent, reproachful vigils, endless reading of the names of the Americans killed in the war, candlelight processions, church services, and, in some cities, larger meetings where

politicians spoke in muted terms. The extremes of citizen opposition to the war were [coming] together, and whatever radical impulse strayed about the fringes of these gatherings was submerged in a spirit of civic solidarity and common enterprise. The largest turnout was in Boston, where a crowd of one hundred thousand, most of them students from the many local colleges, assembled under a warm October sun to hear Senator George McGovern speak; the *Boston Globe* headlined the event as a POLITICAL WOODSTOCK ON THE

The Weathermen's Days of Rage

By October 1969, the SDS, the original New Left organization, collapsed as a result of infighting and the differing goals of members. In its place arose a violent revolutionary youth movement known as the Weathermen. (The group took its name from the Bob Dylan song "Subterranean Homesick Blues," which points out that "You don't need a weatherman to know which way the wind blows.")

In *Reunion: A Memoir,* Tom Hayden discusses the feelings of those who created the Weathermen:

> What was needed was not a Vietnam moratorium, but an extension of the war itself [in America] "behind enemy lines." It was past time to "realign" the Democratic party, it was time to smash it. . . . Armageddon . . . was coming, they said, and it would have to be met with attacks on property, disruption of the repressive government, formation of an underground, and finally armed conflict.

During the trial of the Chicago Seven, the Weathermen sponsored an event called the "Days

of Rage." Although the gathering attracted only a few hundred people—small by '60s standards—the Weathermen, according to Hayden, went on a "wild rampage" through the streets of Chicago, "running through the [well-to-do] Gold Coast [neighborhood], smashing expensive cars and shop windows. It was the beginning of three days of steady rampages, which would shock the city. . . . On the first night alone, three Weathermen were shot. By the end, three hundred were arrested, dozens were badly injured."

The Weathermen changed their name to the Weather Underground and soon took to bombing army research labs and other such targets on campuses. Between January 1969 and April 1970, an estimated five thousand bombings were attributed to the Weather Underground. Although they were planned to injure research papers and equipment, not people, one student was killed at the University of Wisconsin Army Mathematics Research Center.

The large majority of the antiwar movement activists were appalled by the antics of the Weather Underground and spoke out against their violent tactics.

COMMON. But the mellow mood emerged from deeper in the American past. For one twenty-four-hour period the antiwar movement became as American as the Stars and Stripes. The mood of the day was not unlike an old-fashioned, small-town Memorial Day or Fourth of July celebration: solemn, joyous, and, for many, patriotic. Stewart Udall, former Secretary of the Interior, thought the day had the feeling of "a great town meeting.". . . And the crowd saluted with cheers usually reserved for holiday fireworks a skywriting plane that marked out a perfect peace symbol on the cloudless sky blue slate overhead.

What began as a day of student protest spilled out into the adult community. Fifty congressmen and other leaders from the world of politics and diplomacy set out on multiple speaking assignments. Clergy, doctors, and lawyers were caught up in the events. A crowd of twenty thousand gathered on Wall Street to hear Bill Moyers, once an assistant in the Johnson White House. An after-work rally in Bryant Park was jammed with people who left Times Square traffic hopelessly snarled as they marched [several blocks east] to the site. Mayor Lindsay decreed the day a day of mourning and ordered the city's flags to be at half-staff. In Washington, as the day's light dwindled, Coretta Scott King addressed a crowd of thirty thousand before leading a can-

dlelight procession past the White House gates. The soft refrain of "Give Peace a Chance" [by former Beatle John Lennon] was repeated over and over as the solemn marchers, three or four abreast, reached the Nixon abode. "The whole world is watching. Why aren't you?" one marcher cried out. A presidential spokesman declined comment on Mr. Nixon's mood.[69]

The March Against Death

Vietnam Moratorium Day was followed November 13–15, 1969, by a rally held by a national group called the New Mobilization, or New Mobe. This demonstration was billed as a March Against Death and held to honor those who had died in the Vietnam War. A flier handed out by the New Mobe at high schools and colleges across the country explained the purpose of the march:

The New Mobilization Committee to End the War in Vietnam is calling the American people to Washington, D.C., to March Against Death in Vietnam, and to demonstrate for life; for an immediate and unconditional withdrawal of all U.S. troops from Vietnam; for self-determination for Vietnam and black America; for an end to poverty and racism. . . .

At midnight, Nov. 13, the first of fifty state delegations totaling 43,000–45,000 persons will begin walking from

Arlington National [military] Cemetery in a solemn single-file procession past the White House to the steps of the Capitol. There will be at least as many people in each state delegation as the number of slaughtered G.I.s from that state; there will be additional people representing the cities and towns of Vietnam that have been destroyed. The marchers will be wearing placards with the name of either a dead G.I. or a Vietnamese city or town, and as he passes the White House, each person will call out the name on his placard.[70]

For two nights and one day, through bitter cold and pouring rain, twelve-hundred marchers an hour passed the White House, each calling out a name. In this manner, it took almost thirty-eight hours for all of the forty-five thousand marchers to pass the White House.

The finale of the march was held on November 15. This event attracted 250,000 people—the largest political march in U.S. history at that time. (The number 250,000 was the official government estimate; organizers claimed that the event brought 800,000 people, or "two Woodstocks," to Washington.) The crowd filled the park around the Washington Monument, marched past the White House, and ended near the Lincoln Memorial on the Mall. Despite several hundred radicals who advocated storming the White House, the event was said to resemble a homecoming rally on a crisp autumn day, with parents, children,

and teens marching together. Few people were arrested, and there was little violence. Together with the Vietnam Day Moratorium, the two peaceful rallies were good publicity for the antiwar movement, showing prowar forces that the antiwar activists could be patriotic and make their case peacefully.

A crowd of 250,000 surrounds the Washington Monument in Washington, D.C., on November 15, 1969.

Kent State and the ROTC Issue

The politics of protest had a wide-ranging effect on student beliefs as the '60s came to a close. A Gallup poll of college students found that 37 percent considered themselves extremely liberal politically. And for the first time a national poll stated that "campus unrest" was the second biggest problem in America, right behind the war itself. These attitudes were mirrored at Kent State University, a small college south of Cleveland, Ohio, where about 50 percent of the school's twenty-one thousand students opposed the war in Vietnam.

Kent's enrollment had swelled in the 1960s as hundreds of young men jokingly said that, to avoid the draft, they decided to attend KSU rather than VCU (Vietcong University). In addition to attracting students with antiwar beliefs, the college was a favorite of hippies and known as a "party school"; 80 percent of the students there said they had smoked marijuana.

In the late 1960s the focus of protest at Kent State was the Reserve Officers Training Corps, or ROTC, a nationwide program that trained college students to become military officers. In 1970, 50 percent of all army officers were ROTC graduates. ROTC classes were run by the military, not by the individual school. Dougan and Lipsman report the dissatisfaction with this arrangement: "Moderate students and faculty were often disturbed by the requirement that ROTC students receive academic credit despite the fact that the university had no control over the ap-

pointment of professors or the content of classes." Building on this issue, SDS spread the idea that, by inducing college administrators to evict ROTC from their campuses, students would be depriving the army of leadership in Vietnam. Dougan and Lipsman continue,

> The anti-ROTC movement was among the most successful launched by the antiwar activists. Particularly at "elite" institutions like Yale, Harvard, and Stanford, the argument of moderates, that ROTC violated the norms of academic standards, proved persuasive. At those campuses and several others, ROTC was downgraded to the status of "extracurricular activity." Since this was repugnant to the armed forces, the programs were disbanded.

> At the vast majority of college campuses ROTC was not abolished, but enrollments plunged more than two-thirds.[71]

It was in this antimilitary atmosphere that President Nixon announced on Thursday, April 30, 1970, that American and South Vietnamese troops had invaded Cambodia. Predictably, student protest erupted on college campuses across the country. According to Anderson, "Nixon had promised students that he would not enlarge the war by invading the neighbors of South Vietnam, claimed that he was winding down the war, but then he expanded it into Cambodia."[72]

The Kent State Shootings

At Kent State, a demonstration was held the next day calling for the end of ROTC on campus and an immediate U.S. withdrawal from Cambodia. Rallies were planned for the entire weekend, and that Friday night the citizens of Kent were tense as students drank in bars and blocked streets, building bonfires to protest the expansion of the war in Cambodia.

The next day, Ohio governor James Rhodes ordered National Guard troops to Kent. Dougan and Lipsman report on the following events:

The university attempted to keep matters in control on Saturday night by providing live bands in campus dormitories. Early in the evening a crowd began to form on the campus commons. "They're trying to keep the kids penned up in the dorms," shouted one young man. "Let's go." The crowd moved past the dorms, picking up more students as it went along. Nearly 1,000 students approached the ROTC building. . . . Rocks and ignited flares struck the building; it began to burn. When firemen arrived, demonstrators slashed the hoses and threw rocks. The firemen retreated and the building continued to burn.

Finally campus police arrived in riot gear and dispersed the crowd with tear gas. Informed of the situation, [Kent mayor Leroy] Satrom called in the National Guard. A later survey showed that 82 percent of the student body felt that the burning of the ROTC building was either "not at all justified" or "minimally justified." Most also believed that the burning was a means of protesting . . . the Cambodian invasion.[73]

After the ROTC building burned, Rhodes declared a state of emergency and banned demonstrations on campus. The next day, Sunday, a 9:00 P.M. curfew was imposed in Kent. Student leaders arranged to meet with Satrom and the university's president Bob White to demand that the curfew end and that the National Guard leave campus. The mayor promised a meeting but never arrived. Feeling betrayed by the mayor, angry protesters began to throw rocks at soldiers and police. As tear gas wafted across campus, students planned a rally the next day, May 4, at noon.

Classes were held as usual on Monday morning, but in spite of the governor's ban on rallies, about eighty-four hundred students—40 percent of the student population—descended on the commons at 12:00 P.M. While protesters yelled "Pigs off campus,"[74] the Guard launched tear gas canisters at the crowd. Students ran off in all directions with their eyes watering profusely from the CS gas. One contingent of guardsmen had chased a group of about two hundred students who responded by throwing a volley of rocks. The guardsmen retreated as onlookers cheered. Without warning, several of the guardsmen turned back to the crowd. One soldier fired his rifle. He was quickly joined by others as a thirteen-second barrage of gunfire followed. When the shooting stopped nine students were wounded, some critically. Four others lay dead. According to *A Nation Divided:*

> Two of the dead, Jeffrey Miller and Allison Krause, had actively participated in the rally. A third, William Schroeder, an ROTC cadet, had spent the weekend in a moral struggle over his increasing misgivings about the war. He had also attended the rally, but a photograph shows him leaving the area just as the

bullet struck him. The fourth victim, Sandy Scheuer, was merely passing by on her way to class.[75]

On May 14, at Jackson State College in Mississippi, another rally was held to protest Nixon's invasion of Cambodia. Anderson writes, "White state troopers . . . opened fire on black students, shooting 300 bullets into a dormitory, wounding 12 and killing two coeds who were watching events from their window.[76]

Onlookers react with horror at the sight of a female Kent State student shot and killed by National Guardsmen during the protest on May 4, 1970.

Later the President's Commission on Campus Unrest wrote about the shootings at Kent State: "It was the moment when the nation had been driven to use the weapons of war upon its youth."[77]

A National Strike

Even before the bullets were fired at Kent and Jackson State, student leaders across the country reacted strongly when the Cambodian invasion was announced. Before the weekend was out, there were riots at Stanford and strikes at Columbia, Princeton, Notre Dame, the University of Pennsylvania and elsewhere. Zaroulis and Sullivan write,

> The National Student Association and the leaders of the . . . Moratorium called for a nation-wide university strike to begin immediately. . . . Within hours of the call more than one hundred colleges and universities had announced their participation; in the next few weeks— the last weeks of spring term—over 80 percent of the nation's colleges and universities announced some kind of strike action.[78]

After the shootings, 35 college presidents called for an end to the war in Cambodia and 225 student body presidents called for Nixon's impeachment. Meanwhile, on May 9, more than 130,000 students traveled to Washington to protest the Cambodian invasion. That night, Nixon told reporters that "[Students] are [saying] that we ought to get out of Vietnam. I agree with everything that they are trying to accomplish."[79]

In one of the more unusual incidents of the era, Nixon, who could not sleep that night, left the White House at 4:30 A.M. without Secret Service guards—and without the briefcase containing nuclear launch codes that accompanies presidents everywhere they go. Nixon had his valet drive him to the Lincoln Memorial at 5:00 A.M., where a few activists were sleeping. Nixon delivered a short, rambling monologue to thirty startled protesters, the details of which have been lost to history.

The invasion of Cambodia itself did little to change the immediate course of the war. Through their spy networks, the Vietcong knew the Americans were coming and fled into the jungles. Meanwhile, the Nixon administration instituted a new crackdown on the protest movement. Anderson writes, "[The] administration . . . expanded its covert activities against the [antiwar] movement, directing not only agents of the FBI and CIA but also the U.S. Armed Forces, National Security Agency, and Internal Revenue Service to conduct additional wiretappings, surveillance, disinformation, even 'surreptitious entry,' a euphemism for burglary."[80]

By the end of 1970, 335,000 Americans were stationed in Vietnam. During that year, 4,221 were killed and 30,643 were wounded.

Chapter 5

The End of the War: 1971–1973

In early 1971, a Gallup poll found that 44 percent of students agreed that "violence is sometimes justified to bring about change in American society."[81] This was opposed to only 14 percent of nonstudents who supported such a statement. In spite of the poll's findings, however, campuses remained generally calm after the strikes that followed the Kent State shootings in 1970. But Nixon's choice to invade Cambodia turned even more Americans away from supporting the war. And antiwar sentiment was becoming rampant within the military as well.

Dissent Within the Ranks

By 1971, the men who were fighting the war were as polarized as the American public. The army was experiencing unprecedented problems within its ranks. Mirroring civilian society, drug abuse, racial conflicts, and disrespect for authority had become rampant. Retired marine Mike McCain recalled his drug use in Vietnam in the book *Winter Soldiers: An Oral History of Vietnam Veterans Against the War* edited by Richard Stacewicz:

> My first introduction to drugs was in Vietnam. I started smoking reefers there, speed, barbituates [*sic*], because there were times on operations where you didn't want to go to sleep so the corpsman would give us a thousand-tab[let] jar of . . . straight meth amphetamine.[82]

Antiwar sentiment also fueled insubordination among the ranks. Joe Urgo, who served in the air force recalls, "The attitude among the troops was so rebellious that nobody was wearing their helmets anymore. . . . It was all part of our protest to end the war. It was like we had an antiwar mood growing in the barracks. I can tell you, it got so serious . . . that there was a discussion about killing one sergeant."[83]

As the war dragged on, drug use became widespread among soldiers in Vietnam.

A new word crept into army lexicon: The practice of killing officers by rolling hand grenades under their cots became known as "fragging," and those who were believed to make a practice of ordering their troops to take unjustified risks could quickly become victims. Retired marine

Joel Greenberg recalls, "At the end of [1968], they had what they called the 'Mad Grenadier' running around battalion headquarters. . . . This was somebody or somebodies who were throwing grenades and claymores [mines] at the officers."[84]

Army private Pete Zastrow adds, "We were in one place where we had two brigades, and one of the two commanders couldn't stay in his office because people kept opening his door and throwing grenades under his desk."[85]

In addition, desertions rose to unparalleled levels as more than twenty-five thousand soldiers—more than 5 percent—went AWOL (absent without leave) between 1969 and 1973. At the peak of the problem, one soldier was deserting his post every six minutes.

When these veterans were released from the army, they came back to a country that had changed dramatically. Race riots and antiwar protests had become common occurrences; high-profile assassinations seemed to follow each other in quick succession. Thousands of GIs who had seen the horrors of the Vietnam War up close decided to join the ranks of the antiwar demonstrators. A group called Vietnam Veterans Against the War (VVAW) attracted thousands of new members. Former army private Jack McCloskey explained his reasons for joining the VVAW:

[We] made promises to dead people. The only way we could justify the deaths of our buddies over there was by saying, "We've got to stop it." We've got to stop it. Stop the killing. Stop the killing. [Tearfully.] Here in San Francisco [at antiwar demonstrations], that was the chant I remember hearing the most, "Stop the killing, stop the killing, stop the killing."[86]

Operation Dewey Canyon III

In April 1971, the government braced for what had become an annual spring ritual—the antiwar march on Washington. This spring, however, the usual hippies, college students, and professors were joined for the first time by large numbers of the VVAW. By April 1971, membership in the VVAW had swelled to 12,000—up from only six hundred one year earlier.

The vets staged an April 19 event called Operation Dewey Canyon III. (Dewey Canyon I had been the code name for the secret marine operation in Laos in 1969. Dewey Canyon II was the code name for the South Vietnamese invasion of Laos in 1971.) For Dewey Canyon III, about fifteen-hundred vets, according to one VVAW spokesman, "staged a five-day 'invasion' of Washington, D.C., 'a limited incursion into the country of Congress.'"[87]

The vets descended on Washington for four days of protest. After enduring severe hardships in Vietnam, the vets adamantly opposed the war. Army veteran and protester Bill Branson recalled the attitudes of his fellow protesters:

Two Vietnam War veteran amputees are rolled down the steps of the U.S. Supreme Court building on April 22, 1971, during Dewey Canyon III.

We were incredibly militant. We figured if we were going to go all the way out there to Washington, to the belly of the beast, we were going to kick some ass. And we did. . . .

We didn't want to tear the place apart, but we definitely wanted to make an impression. We were not there to do anything halfway. As we got together in bigger and bigger groups, we became more militant. . . .

We marched up Pennsylvania Avenue [past the White House] and people came out everywhere. Buildings emptied. . . . There were lots and lots of tourists there, and they were . . . cheering. We had people running out shaking hands. I had never been in a march like this. . . .

There was cops along the sides of the street, but they stayed away from us. I can guarantee you, if they had attacked us then, there would have been guerilla warfare in the streets. . . . They wouldn't have been able to stop us. Guys [who had fought in Vietnam] were not going to put up with [anything].[88]

In the White House, Nixon claimed that the marchers were just radical hippies, not real Vietnam vets. To counter this assertion, a reporter counted about one thousand military service cards carried by the men that proved that the soldiers were

veterans. Nixon's statement was discredited the next day in newspapers.

The Justice Department issued an injunction preventing the vets from camping on the Mall near the Capitol. An appeal by the VVAW to overturn this decision quickly made its way to the Supreme Court, which backed the Justice Department. In spite of the injunction, the vets camped there anyway. The vets had the sympathy of the police, however, and veteran Barry Romo recalls what happened that night: "This . . . old, chubby [policeman], looks down on us and goes, 'I don't see anybody sleeping. [Laughs.] Nobody sleeping here. You guys don't have to worry about nothing because we don't see anything and we're not going to do anything.'"[89] The next day, the headlines in the *Washington Star* read "Vets Overrule Supreme Court."[90]

During the week of Dewey Canyon III, the vets lobbied congressmen to end the war and held mock skirmishes based on real battles in Vietnam on the steps of the Capitol. *A Nation Divided* recalls the climax of the event:

The most moving protest, however, came on Friday, April 23, the final day of Dewey Canyon III. Marching to the steps of the Capitol, veterans came up against a barrier erected to stop them. They halted and one by one hurled medals they had won in Vietnam over the barrier and onto the steps of the Capitol Building. . . .

Many of the veterans embraced each other and broke into tears.[91]

The veterans of Vietnam added an undeniable credibility to the antiwar movement, according to Danny Friedman, who served from 1967 to 1969:

> We gave legitimacy to the antiwar movement. The antiwar movement were considered a bunch of commies and peaceniks until the veterans got involved. To say that it didn't have an impact is like saying the sun doesn't have an impact on the temperature of the earth. It totally took the antiwar movement from a bunch of radical college kids, who people thought were terrorists, to the sons of America, and America started noticing. We were working-class kids who fought the war and came back. That was the bottom line. America, your sons have come home and are telling you, Hey, wake up and smell the roses. This is what really happened over there. We're not no college professors or commies. We're the guys that were there.[92]

The Pentagon Papers

A majority of those who supported the war doubted the horror stories told by the vets during the Washington march. But a series of articles in the *New York Times* soon exposed the American public to more than twenty years of official government deceptions concerning Vietnam. On Sunday, June 13, 1971, the *Times* began publishing a series of articles called "Vietnam Archive," based on a top-secret government study that would later become known as the Pentagon Papers.

The Pentagon Papers consisted of four thousand government documents gathered from the CIA, the National Security Agency, the White House, and the Departments of State and Defense. These documents were accompanied by three thousand pages of narrative text that filled forty-seven volumes. The highly classified papers were copied by a former prowar adviser named Daniel Ellsberg, who smuggled them out of the RAND Corporation research institute, where they were compiled. After reading the papers, Ellsberg changed his mind about the war, and secretly turned over, or "leaked," the information to the *Times*.

The Pentagon Papers were compiled at the beginning of June 1967 at the request of Secretary of Defense Robert McNamara. They covered the history of American involvement in Vietnam from 1945 to March 1968. In an introduction to a book of the papers published later, Mike Gravel, a Democratic senator from Alaska, called the Pentagon Papers

> the most complete study yet performed of the policy-making process that led to our deepening involvement in Vietnam, and the most revealing insight we have had into the functioning of our government's national security appara-

Copies of the Pentagon Papers are distributed to the press. The Pentagon Papers were classified government documents detailing American involvement in Vietnam.

tus. . . . The Papers prove that, from the beginning, the war has been an American war, serving only to perpetuate American military power in Asia . . . as the leaders of America sought to preserve their reputation for toughness and determination. . . .

No one who reads this study can fail to conclude that, had the true . . . facts been made known earlier, the war would long ago have ended, and the needless deaths of hundreds of thousands of Americans and Vietnamese would have been averted. This is the great lesson of the Pentagon Papers.[93]

After reading all forty-seven volumes of the Pentagon Papers, Tom Hayden wrote his own short summation:

1. The United States was in Vietnam mainly to preserve an image of strength. . . .

3. The U.S. government was planning military action in 1964, even while Lyndon Johnson was pledging "no wider war."

4. The United States was fighting against a popular-based nationalist movement.

5. U.S. planning was indifferent to human factors. The document included any number of . . . observations like this 1966 one [showing U.S. indifference to civilian casualties]: "By shallow-flooding the rice, it leads after time to widespread starvation (more than a million?).[94]

When the *Times* published the papers, Nixon was livid. He instructed his aide John Ehrlichman to put together a team of undercover agents called the Plumbers to stop such "leaks" of information to the press. This group broke into the offices of Ellsberg's psychiatrist, where they had hoped to find information that would discredit the researcher. In addition, the Justice Department quickly indicted Ellsberg on several serious felony charges, including theft, espionage, and conspiracy. The charges were dismissed in 1973 when it was revealed that Nixon had ordered illegal wiretaps and burglaries against Ellsberg and offered the judge in the case the directorship of the FBI.

In the weeks after the papers were published, a Gallup poll showed that 61 percent of Americans favored an immediate U.S. end to the war in Vietnam.

The Politics of Peace

Ironically, as more Americans agreed that the United States should pull out of Viet-

nam, the American peace movement itself was becoming more fractured and less effective. Black and white activists disagreed over matters of race, while new elements of women's liberation and gay rights organizations fought with the white heterosexual males who had been running the antiwar groups for years. The "Evict Nixon" rally held in Washington in October 1971 attracted fewer than one thousand people. When eight hundred marchers attempted to enter the White House with a notice that said "WE THE PEOPLE HEREBY SERVE NOTICE OF OUR DETERMINATION TO EVICT YOU FROM PUBLIC OFFICE,"[95] about three hundred were arrested.

On November 6, 1971, antiwar demonstrations in San Francisco drew 40,000; New York, 30,000; Boston, 10,000. Although these rallies were large, the crowds were only a fraction of the size of previous years.

Politics, not peace marches, were attracting the public's attention by early 1972. Assistant to President Nixon for national security affairs Henry Kissinger had been negotiating with the North Vietnamese with limited success for several years. And the United States had reduced the number of troops in Vietnam from 335,000 in 1970 to 140,000 by the end of 1971. With more GIs coming home, and fewer soldiers being killed and wounded, a majority of the American public felt that Nixon was bringing a successful conclusion to the war.

The year 1972 was a presidential election year, and in spite of the Pentagon

The White House "Plumbers"

The Pentagon Papers consisted of forty-seven volumes of official government documents that exposed the American effort in Vietnam as futile and wasteful. When researcher Daniel Ellsberg "leaked" the information in the Pentagon Papers to the press in 1971, the Nixon White House put together a team of men known as the Plumbers to stop the "leaks."

The Plumbers, led by Egil Krogh Jr., included Charles Colson, E. Howard Hunt, and G. Gordon Liddy. These men broke into the office of Ellsberg's psychiatrist in a futile attempt to discover confidential records that would discredit Ellsberg. Later the group assaulted Ellsberg at an antiwar rally.

In June 1972, the Plumbers broke in to the Democratic National Headquarters at the Watergate Office Complex in an attempt to find documents that would help Nixon defeat George McGovern, his opponent in the 1972 presidential race.

Although Nixon was reelected, the discovery of the Watergate break-in—a minor, if sleazy affair—was to prove to be his undoing. The president resigned in August 1974, and Vice President Gerald R. Ford was sworn in to complete the term.

Daniel Ellsberg (shown here with his wife), the former prowar adviser who "leaked" the Pentagon Papers to the press.

Papers, Nixon's standing remained high with the American public. (The harassment against Ellsberg and the Watergate break-in would not be revealed for another year.) In February 1972, Nixon bolstered his status as a statesman when he visited the People's Republic of China where he met with Chinese leader Mao Tse-tung, and opened political, business, and cultural relations between the United States and Communist China for the first time. In May, Nixon met with leaders in the Soviet Union. Nixon's meetings created a better understanding between the superpower nations, although the Chinese and Soviet Communists continued to support the North Vietnamese and the war would soon heat up again.

A New Wave of Protest

At the beginning of April, North Vietnam invaded the south in a renewed assault, and on April 15 Nixon ordered massive U.S. bombing attacks on the North Vietnamese capital Hanoi and the port of Haiphong for the first time since 1968. This move brought the battered peace movement back into action, and eight hundred people attended a hastily called demonstration in Washington.

As the bombings increased in Vietnam, smaller decentralized protests at college campuses took the place of large mass protests. Violence once again broke out at schools across the country on April 17, when three thousand rock-throwing students fought with police in Madison, Wisconsin; fifteen hundred surrounded the

federal building in San Francisco; and five hundred Columbia students closed down city streets in New York. On April 18, two thousand Harvard students attacked the Center for International Affairs where Kissinger had once worked. The protesters

The Women's Liberation Movement

Inspired by the civil rights and antiwar movements, thousands of women who had protested the war in the early 1970s began to agitate for equal rights, equal education, and better pay. Almost forty thousand women gathered in New York to celebrate the fiftieth anniversary of the 1920 passage of the Nineteenth Amendment, which gave women the right to vote. It was the first large-scale women's march in fifty years. Demonstrations were also held in San Francisco, Boston, Los Angeles, Denver, Baltimore, Seattle, and Washington, D.C.

The women's liberation movement was initially much more successful than the antiwar movement. The National Organization for Women (NOW) quickly grew to forty thousand members in seven hundred chapters nationwide within three years of the first rally. By 1971, Congress was debating whether to add the proposed Equal Rights Amendment to the Constitution. In 1971, a women's organization sued 350 universities for sex discrimination. NOW sued the public school systems across the country for discriminating against women in pay and promotions. Women demanded equal employment in more than thirteen hundred national corporations that received federal funds. State laws that limited birth control and abortion were also overturned. In 1972, feminist Gloria Steinem founded *Ms.* magazine, and circulation soon reached 200,000 copies a month.

As Terry H. Anderson writes in *The Movement and the Sixties,* "The early 1970s became a Feminist Renaissance."

broke windows, smashed furniture, set small fires, destroyed research papers, and spray-painted obscenities on the walls.

On April 21 a general strike was called for all American colleges and universities. Although most demonstrations remained peaceful, violence continued at many campuses. Zaroulis and Sullivan documented several of the disturbances:

At Princeton 350 students seized the building of the Woodrow Wilson School for Public and International Affairs. . . . At Stanford over 100 students were arrested for blocking highways; previously they had attacked an electronics lab which, they said, did war-related research. At the University of Michigan students attacked an ROTC building, vandalizing its offices; later 1,500 of them roamed through Ann Arbor, tying up traffic for four hours. At Boston University 1,500 students attacked the administration building, smashing doors, taking files, ripping out telephones; the next day 40 students took over the office of the dean of students. At the University of Texas at Austin police dispersed demonstrators with tear gas and nightsticks. Twenty-seven students were arrested at Syracuse University while barricading the entrance to an air force recruiting office; 15 were arrested at Idaho's Boise State University. . . . At Columbia, 500 students rallied and then, chanting and singing (falling silent as they passed hospitals) and carrying Viet

Cong and Cuban and black nationalist flags, marched downtown via Broadway to the Veterans Administration building. . . . At the midday campus rally, blacks joined whites for the first time in that spring's demonstrations. Many of the white speakers welcomed them with contrition, criticizing themselves for not fighting in the black "revolution."[96]

On April 22, antiwar demonstrations were held across the United States and across much of Western Europe and Canada. Turnout at the U.S. rallies, however, was at an all-time low. Only thirty-five thousand marched in New York, thirty thousand in San Francisco, and twelve thousand in Los Angeles. A May 4 demonstration marking the second anniversary of the Kent State shootings only drew about one thousand in New York and smaller crowds elsewhere. It seemed as if Americans were as tired of the antiwar movement as they were of the war itself.

Around that time, as the North Vietnamese continued to advance into the south, Nixon ordered the mining of all northern ports and the bombing of all railroads that went to China. This set off a new wave of campus protest and violence in Boulder, Colorado; Minneapolis, Minnesota; Albuquerque, New Mexico; Gainesville, Florida; Athens, Ohio; and at other smaller colleges. Meanwhile, a *New York Times* poll showed that 59 percent of Americans backed Nixon's actions in Vietnam as a way to end the war.

Public turnout for antiwar demonstrations reached record lows toward the end of the war.

New Problems for Americans

By January 1972 the conflict in Vietnam had been going on for almost seven years. The United States was continuing massive air strikes on North and South Vietnam along with Laos and Cambodia. In spite of this bombing campaign, more and more ground troops were being brought home, which helped boost Nixon's popularity in the public opinion polls. Another 75,000 troops were withdrawn from Vietnam by May 1, 1972, leaving only 65,000, as compared to 335,000 in 1970.

With the troops coming home, new problems were facing millions of Americans. The Pentagon had been spending billions of dollars to buy weapons, and when the war slowed, defense factories closed all over the country, causing hundreds of thousands of Americans to lose their high-paying factory jobs. According to *A Nation Divided,* "more than 230,000 jobs were lost in the aircraft and helicopter industries alone, while the decline of troop strength in Vietnam put more veterans than ever before into the job market."[97] As a result, veterans returning home found it difficult to find jobs to ease their return to civilian life. In addition, men who went to college to avoid the draft created a glut of college graduates in the early 1970s. People who were unemployed, laid off, or searching for jobs to support their families had more pressing concerns than the situation in Vietnam. They wanted the war to end, but few had concrete ideas about how this might be accomplished.

The Last Protest

In the summer of 1972, the country once again geared up for a presidential election. The Democrats nominated South Dakota senator George McGovern as the "peace candidate" who promised to end the war immediately. His platform was supported by 61 percent of all Americans, but support for Nixon was equally widespread.

The high numbers of troops coming home from Vietnam often had difficulties finding jobs.

The last protest of the Vietnam War came in August 1972 at the Republican convention in Miami Beach. By now the movement was shrinking rapidly. Only three to four thousand people protested at the convention; significantly, about one-third were Vietnam veterans in the VVAW. As Nixon gave his acceptance speech in the convention center, about one thousand protesters were arrested outside.

Inside the convention hall, three badly wounded vets held up a sign that said "Stop the War." One of those vets was paraplegic Ron Kovic, who had been shot in the spine in Vietnam in 1965 at the age of nineteen. Kovic, paralyzed from the chest down, began to speak out against war in 1970. Sitting in his wheelchair, with his chest decorated with medals he had won during the war, Kovic had been a popular speaker at antiwar rallies—and a photogenic subject for the television news. Kovic's autobiography, *Born on the Fourth of July,* was made into a movie by director Oliver Stone in 1991. In the book, Kovic recalled his dramatic protest inside the Republican convention:

President Nixon began to speak and all three of us took a deep breath and shouted at the top of our lungs, "Stop the bombing, stop the war, stop the bombing, stop the war," as loud and as hard as we could, looking directly at Nixon. The security agents immediately threw up their arms, trying to hide us from the cameras and the pres-

ident. "Stop the bombing, stop the bombing," I screamed. For an instant [Walter] Cronkite looked down, then turned his head away. They're not going to show it [on television], I thought. They're going to try and hide us like they did in the hospitals. Hundreds of people around us began to clap and shout "Four more years [of Nixon]," trying to drown out our protest. They all seemed very angry and shouted at us to stop. We continued shouting, interrupting Nixon again and again until Secret Service agents grabbed our chairs from behind and began pulling us backward as fast as they could out of the convention hall. . . .

"So this is how they treat the wounded veterans!" I screamed. A short guy with a big FOUR MORE YEARS button ran up to me and spat in my face. "Traitor!" he screamed, as he was yanked back by police. Pandemonium was breaking out all around us and the Secret Service men kept pulling us out backward.

"I served two tours of duty in Vietnam!" I screamed to one newsman. "I gave three-quarters of my body for America. And what do I get! Spit in the face" I kept screaming until we hit the side entrance where the agents pushed us outside and shut the doors, locking them with chains and padlocks so reporters wouldn't be able to follow us out for interviews. . . .

I sat in my [wheel]chair still shaking and began to cry.[98]

Ignoring Kovic's dramatic protest and the agitation of those outside the convention hall, Nixon pledged that he would bring all ground troops in Vietnam home by Christmas. With the war issue off the agenda for most Americans, Nixon garnered more than 61 percent of the vote in November, carrying forty-nine of fifty states in the electoral college, defeating McGovern by a wide margin.

The war issue was by no means resolved, however, and in December 1972, the United States dropped more bombs on Hanoi than ever before. By the end of 1972, Nixon—true to his word—had brought home a majority of ground forces in Vietnam, leaving only twenty-four thousand military personnel behind.

The War Is Over!

In early 1973, Nixon announced that a cease-fire would commence in Vietnam on January 27. On that day, the military draft ended in the United States, and the U.S. commitment in Vietnam, which began in 1954, finally ended. In February and March, 590 American prisoners of war (POWs) returned to the United States.

A photo dated February 15, 1973 shows the liberation of American POWs in Hanoi, North Vietnam.

The final statistics of the war were startling: During the seven-year war, 3,330,000 Americans served in Vietnam, 58,183 were killed, and 307,713 were wounded. In addition, an estimated 3 million Vietnamese were killed, along with hundreds of thousands in Laos and Cambodia. The war had cost the United States $150 billion, and the United States had dropped three times more bombs on the tiny country of Vietnam than it had in all of World War II.

On April 30, 1975, following the hasty evacuation by some one thousand Americans and six thousand South Vietnamese sympathizers, North Vietnamese troops entered Saigon, and North and South Vietnam were reunited as one country under a Communist system that would remain in place into the twenty-first century. In Cambodia, the government was destabilized from American invasion, allowing Communist leader Pol Pot to gain control of that country. His Khmer Rouge followers killed an estimated 1.5 million Cambodians in the following decade.

After the War

When the war ended, the antiwar movement, which was never unified as one solid organization, quickly dispersed. In the next several years, economic problems replaced political ones as inflation spiraled out of control and gas prices doubled almost overnight. Nixon's abuse of presidential power in the Watergate break-in had been exposed and he resigned on August 9, 1974, to avoid certain impeachment. By

the mid-1970s, the country was mired in economic crisis, and the U.S. loss in Viet-

Problems of Returning Veterans

Many Vietnam veterans faced physical and psychological problems when they returned home. According to Richard Stacewicz in *Winter Soldiers,* an estimated one in four Vietnam vets (and about half of all combat vets) have been diagnosed with a condition known as posttraumatic stress disorder (PTSD). This syndrome caused its victims to experience a wide range of problems as they tried to adjust to daily life after fighting in the war.

Sufferers of PTSD were known to experience irritability, depression, a sense of guilt for having survived while others did not, and difficulties in relating to other people. Nightmares, flashbacks to battle scenes, and overreactions to sudden noises were also common. Because of PTSD, some Vietnam vets could not hold down jobs or maintain normal family life. In the 1980s, an estimated 30 percent of homeless people living on American streets were Vietnam vets.

Vets also experienced problems caused by the use of the herbicide Agent Orange. Because this chemical instantly kills plants, U.S. policy makers decided to have it sprayed in great amounts over the jungles of Vietnam. The idea was to strip the leaves from the trees the enemy was using for cover. Few U.S. military personnel were aware that Agent Orange contains dioxin, one of the most toxic chemicals ever synthesized. Later, soldiers who had come into contact with Agent Orange experienced liver and other cancers, immune-deficiency diseases, persistent pain, and other problems. Researchers also noticed that the children of these veterans suffered from birth defects, including gross malformations. After years of appealing to the Veterans Administration, some of the vets exposed to Agent Orange received financial compensation for their problems.

nam was quickly eclipsed by news of more closing factories, soaring unemployment, and gasoline shortages. The only people who continued to think about Vietnam seemed to be the vets who returned home with a host of problems caused by the war.

The end of the war also signaled the death of the counterculture era which lasted from 1964 to 1972. As Jerry Rubin wrote in *Growing Up at 37,*

> Creativity fell off in all areas of life—from music to art to writing. The Beatles broke up [in 1970]. Hippie communities like Haight-Ashbury became ghost towns. Those who said "burn down the school" one year enrolled as students the next. The psychological depression of 1970 to 1973 preceded the economic depression of 1975.
>
> The economic pinch drove protesters back into the system to survive. Beards came off, and people went back into their fathers' businesses. The next generation saw us as a New Establishment and rebelled against us by going Establishment. The mass movement as we had known it was over. Action brought reactions. . . . To be, to think, to meditate, to feel became greater desires than to do. My role as "do it" catalyst was over.[99]

A War for America's Soul

For years, the White House, FBI, and CIA tried to prove that the antiwar movement was sponsored and directed by Communist infiltrators. Study after study, however, showed that, although there had been some efforts by outside agitators to manipulate idealistic young people, resistance to the war was homegrown and widespread. And those who participated in the antiwar movement continued to believe that their protests permanently changed attitudes against war. Anderson writes,

> The antiwar movement alone did not end U.S. participation in Vietnam, but it did provoke citizens out of cold war allegiance, it generated and focused public opposition, and influenced presidents. . . . Protesters also prompted citizens to [continue to] raise questions about their nation's foreign policy. . . . In this sense then, the antiwar movement was victorious,

for as historian George Herring states: "The conventional wisdom in the military is that the United States won every battle [in Vietnam] but lost the war. It could be said of the antiwar movement that it lost every battle but *eventually* won the war—the war for America's minds and especially for its soul."[100]

Continuing Debate

Whether or not the antiwar movement did win American hearts and souls has been a matter of debate for decades. To those on the prowar side, Vietnam represented a place where basic American ideals were at stake—the United States represented freedom, and Americans would fight and die to support that freedom.

Those in the antiwar movement, however, believed that they were exposing a deep and hypocritical discrepancy between American ideals and government actions. One glaring example in the 1960s was that

A demonstrator holds up an antiwar sign at the 1968 Democratic National Convention in Chicago.

Growing numbers in the civil rights and antiwar movements began by rejecting American practices, went on to reject American ideals, and soon, since America *was* its ideals, rejected the conventional versions of American identity altogether. The early New Left rejected the American political consensus as hypocritical: the country was in default on its promise to recognize equal rights. The later New Left and the black liberation movement rejected the promise as well: the American political consensus was cursed by original sin, it was and had ever been racist and imperial [from its founding], it had long been making its way to [the use of] napalm in the defense of freedom.[101]

Because of the basic distrust of government, which began in the 1960s, almost every president since Richard Nixon has come under intense scrutiny from Congress, the media, and the American people. Several of Jimmy Carter's top officials were forced to resign because of ethical problems, members of the Reagan and Bush administrations came under attack for arranging the sale of weapons to Iran to finance an illegal war in Nicaragua, and Bill Clinton was impeached for lying to a grand jury. Under such circumstances, it is doubtful that any twenty-first century president will be able to muster support for a questionable military action by deliberately misleading the public, as Lyndon Johnson

Americans were fighting to give the Vietnamese democratic elections while African Americans in some parts of the South could not themselves participate in the electoral process. This sort of double standard caused many in the movement to question all American ideals.

Former SDS president Todd Gitlin examines this theme in *The Twilight of Common Dreams*. The concluding flourish is typical of New Left rhetoric from the antiwar protest days.

had done in 1964 after the Gulf of Tonkin incident.

Aid and Comfort to the Enemy?

Since the war ended, some members of the movement have expressed regrets about traveling to North Vietnam and giving "aid and comfort" to the enemy. The antiwar movement clearly boosted the morale of the North Vietnamese, and leaders in Hanoi paid careful attention to the large protests. Long after the last shot was fired in Vietnam, debate continued concerning whether or not the movement prolonged the war.

Many historians believe that the North Vietnamese were ready to hold out as long as possible to achieve their goals, no matter how many tons of bombs the United States dropped on their country. As far as the waving of North Vietnamese flags and the blatant anti-American sentiment expressed by those in the movement, Gitlin writes,

It is important to be clear about what this anti-Americanism of the time was and was not. It was a sentiment more than a commitment, a loathing more than a theory, a yelp of anguish more than an ideology. It was built on disappointment—the crashing of a liberal faith in American goodness, and, as a result, the turning of that faith upside down. The result was that as the war ground on, any lingering New Left belief in [an] American dream . . . held in common, bled away. The climate became . . . inflamed, the disbelief in con-

structive change . . . fierce, and the despair over the course of American policy . . . pervasive. . . . From the early nineteenth century onward, [natives] and immigrants alike had each proclaimed that they were the real Americans, as opposed to those Others [in foreign lands]. Now, for the first time in American history, [the protesters] had no stomach to be included, and wanted out.[102]

One of the architects of the war, Robert S. McNamara, has his own insider's view about why America lost in Vietnam, and it has little to do with the protest movement. In a chapter about lessons learned in Vietnam, the former defense secretary writes,

We underestimated the power of nationalism to motivate a people (in this case, the North Vietnamese and Vietcong) to fight and die for their beliefs and values. . . .

We failed . . . to recognize the limitations of modern, high-technology military equipment, forces, and doctrine in confronting [Vietnam's] unconventional, highly motivated people's movements. . . .

After the action got under way . . . we failed to retain popular support [in America] in part because we did not explain fully what was happening and why we were doing what we did.[103]

Secretary of Defense Robert S. McNamara briefs the press on U.S. and South Vietnamese air strikes against the North Vietnamese in 1965.

The Legacy Today

In 1999 the U.S. Post Office issued commemorative stamps celebrating the 1960s. The series of stamps included well-known images from the '60s such as the first human footprint on the moon, Dr. Martin Luther King Jr. at the Mall in Washington, and a classic '65 Ford Mustang. Above the stamp depicting soldiers in Vietnam is a white dove of peace perched on a guitar neck—the logo from the 1969 Woodstock Music Festival. Below the Vietnam stamp is the peace symbol, which combines two flag signals, of letters N and D, which stands for nuclear disarmament.

This mixture of '60s symbols issued twenty-four years after the last Americans left Vietnam shows how much the world has changed since those turbulent years of protests, riots, and assassinations. In the late 1960s the peace symbol was a provocative statement against the war in Vietnam. Today it is simply a quaint emblem of a time long ago when America went to war in a foreign land—and had to fight another war on college campuses and in the streets of its own cities.

Although the antiwar movement ended with the war, the tactics it made popular have been used by countless other social movements since that time, from the antinuclear marches in the 1980s to the protests against the World Trade Organization in Seattle in 1999.

The antiwar movement left a legacy of people who question authority, who conduct independent research and investigation into government claims, and who use grassroots organizing as a path to a broader audience. The street theater that disrupted the 1999 meeting of members of the World Trade Organization in Seattle looked to many like a flashback to the '60s.

Whether the antiwar movement helped stop the war or prolonged it is no longer the main issue as the Vietnam War fades into history. Although some may question the motives or techniques used by the movement, many of the protesters sacrificed their economic and physical well-being to expose government lies and hypocrisy and to try to stop the slaughter of

At Seattle's 1999 World Trade Organization protest, a demonstrator tries to give a flower to police, echoing earlier antiwar tactics.

people they believed were not a threat to national security. They marched in the cold and the rain; they were beaten and maced by police. Unarmed, they faced down rifle-wielding soldiers, and for some, this act of protest was their last.

As the Pentagon Papers and later investigations into the Gulf of Tonkin inci-

dent, the FBI's *Cointelpro* covert operations program, and the Watergate burglary showed, American decision makers at the highest levels were willing to lie and commit illegal acts to further their own personal agendas. Those in the antiwar movement were often the first to shine the harsh light of reality on these situations. And though it was often painful for the American people to hear the truth, it has also been observed that "the truth shall set you free."

✯ Notes ✯

Introduction: The United States in Vietnam

1. Edward Doyle and Samuel Lipsman, eds., *Setting the Stage*. Boston: Boston Publishing, 1981, p. 37.
2. James William Gibson, "Revisiting Vietnam, Again," *Harper's Magazine*, April 2000, p. 79.
3. Quoted in Clark Dougan and Samuel Lipsman, eds., *A Nation Divided*. Boston: Boston Publishing, 1984, p. 46.
4. Dougan and Lipsman, *A Nation Divided*, p. 46.

Chapter 1: The First Protests: 1962–1965

5. Stewart Burns, *Social Movements of the 1960s*. Boston: Twayne, 1990, p. 57.
6. Burns, *Social Movements of the 1960s*, p. 59.
7. Quoted in James Miller, *"Democracy in the Streets": From Port Huron to the Siege of Chicago*. New York: Simon and Schuster, 1987, p. 221.
8. Peter B. Levy, ed., *America in the Sixties: Right, Left, and Center*. Westport, CT: Praeger, 1998, p. 135.
9. Quoted in Joan Morrison and Robert K. Morrison, eds., *From Camelot to Kent State: The Sixties Expereince in the Words of Those Who Lived It*. New York: Times Books, 1987, p. 226.
10. Burns, *Social Movements of the 1960s*, p. 61.
11. Quoted in Burns, *Social Movements of the 1960s*, p. 63.
12. Jerry Rubin, *Do It!* New York: Ballantine Books, 1970, p. 24.
13. Quoted in Terry H. Anderson, *The Movement and the Sixties*. New York: Oxford University Press, 1995, p. 124.
14. Anderson, *The Movement and the Sixties*, pp. 124–25.
15. Quoted in Miller, *"Democracy in the Streets,"* p. 23.
16. Thomas Powers, *The War at Home*. New York: Grossman, 1973, p. 81.
17. Rubin, *Do It!* p. 38.
18. Quoted in Morrison and Morrison, *From Camelot to Kent State*, p. 280.
19. Rubin, *Do It!* p. 43.
20. Dougan and Lipsman, *A Nation Divided*, pp. 72, 76.
21. Quoted in Dougan and Lipsman, *A Nation Divided*, p. 78.

Chapter 2: The Escalation: 1966–1967

22. Quoted in Robert S. McNamara, *In Retrospect: The Tragedy and Lessons of Vietnam:*

New York: Random House, 1995, p. 160.

23. Powers, *The War at Home,* p. 115.

24. Nancy Zaroulis and Gerald Sullivan, *Who Spoke Up? American Protest Against the War in Vietnam 1963–1975.* Garden City, NY: Doubleday, 1984, p. 82.

25. Quoted in Zaroulis and Sullivan, *Who Spoke Up?* p. 87.

26. Quoted in Zaroulis and Sullivan, *Who Spoke Up?* p. 86.

27. Anderson, *The Movement and the Sixties,* pp. 144–45.

28. Anderson, *The Movement and the Sixties,* p. 151.

29. Zaroulis and Sullivan, *Who Spoke Up?* p. 103.

30. Zaroulis and Sullivan, *Who Spoke Up?* p. 108.

31. Quoted in Zaroulis and Sullivan, *Who Spoke Up?* p. 111.

32. Jane and Michael Stern, *Sixties People.* New York: Alfred A. Knopf, 1990, p. 152.

33. Quoted in Zaroulis and Sullivan, *Who Spoke Up?* p. 136.

34. Zaroulis and Sullivan, *Who Spoke Up?* p. 139.

35. Abbie Hoffman, *Soon to Be a Major Motion Picture.* New York: Perigee Books, 1980, pp. 135–36.

Chapter 3: The Explosive Year: 1968

36. Charles Kaiser, *1968 in America.* New York: Weidenfeld & Nicolson, 1988, p. xv.

37. Anderson, *The Movement and the Sixties,* p. 184.

38. Quoted in Kaiser, *1968 in America,* p. 77.

39. Quoted in Dougan and Lipsman, *A Nation Divided,* p. 104.

40. Dougan and Lipsman, *A Nation Divided,* p. 105.

41. Kaiser, *1968 in America,* pp. 162–63.

42. Zaroulis and Sullivan, *Who Spoke Up?* p. 169.

43. Anderson, *The Movement and the Sixties,* p. 214.

44. Rubin, *Do It!* p. 81.

45. Quoted in Abbie Hoffman, *The Best of Abbie Hoffman.* New York: Four Walls Eight Windows, 1989, p. 52.

46. Hoffman, *Soon to Be a Major Motion Picture,* pp. 144–45.

47. Dougan and Lipsman, *A Nation Divided,* p. 128.

48. Quoted in Anderson, *The Movement and the Sixties,* p. 221.

49. Tom Hayden, *Reunion: A Memoir.* New York: Random House, 1988, pp. 299–300.

50. Quoted in Dougan and Lipsman, *A Nation Divided,* p. 120.

51. Quoted in Anderson, *The Movement and the Sixties,* p. 222.

52. Anderson, *The Movement and the Sixties,* p. 222.

53. Anderson, *The Movement and the Sixties,* pp. 223–24.

54. Kaiser, *1968 in America,* p. 243.

55. Hayden, *Reunion,* p. 321.

56. Quoted in Hayden, *Reunion,* p. 323.

Chapter 4: Days of Rage: 1969–1970

57. Richard Stacewicz, *Winter Soldiers: An Oral History of Vietnam Veterans Against the War.* New York: Twayne, 1997, p. 191.
58. Hayden, *Reunion,* p. 331.
59. Hayden, *Reunion,* p. 331.
60. Hayden, *Reunion,* p. 333.
61. Quoted in Hayden, *Reunion,* p. 334.
62. Quoted in Zaroulis and Sullivan, *Who Spoke Up?* p. 249.
63. Quoted in Zaroulis and Sullivan, *Who Spoke Up?* p. 250.
64. Quoted in Hayden, *Reunion,* p. 339.
65. Hoffman, *Soon to Be a Major Motion Picture,* p. 204.
66. Anderson, *The Movement and the Sixties,* p. 227.
67. Quoted in Hayden, *Reunion,* p. 408.
68. Quoted in Hayden, *Reunion,* p. 452.
69. Quoted in Zaroulis and Sullivan, *Who Spoke Up?* pp. 296–70.
70. Quoted in Irwin Unger and Debi Unger, eds., *The Times Were a Changin': The Sixties Reader.* New York: Three Rivers Press, 1998, pp. 297–98.
71. Dougan and Lipsman, *A Nation Divided,* p. 170.
72. Anderson, *The Movement and the Sixties,* pp. 349–50.
73. Dougan and Lipsman, *A Nation Divided,* p. 171.
74. Quoted in Dougan and Lipsman, *A Nation Divided,* p. 172.
75. Dougan and Lipsman, *A Nation Divided,* p. 172.
76. Anderson, *The Movement in the Sixties,* p. 351.
77. Quoted in Zaroulis and Sullivan, *Who Spoke Up?* p. 319.
78. Quoted in Zaroulis and Sullivan, *Who Spoke Up?* p. 319.
79. Quoted in Zaroulis and Sullivan, *Who Spoke Up?* p. 323.
80. Anderson, *The Movement in the Sixties,* p. 352.

Chapter 5: The End of the War: 1971–1973

81. Quoted in Dougan and Lipsman, *A Nation Divided,* p. 177.
82. Quoted in Stacewicz, *Winter Soldiers,* p. 148.
83. Quoted in Stacewicz, *Winter Soldiers,* p. 127.
84. Quoted in Stacewicz, *Winter Soldiers,* p. 133.
85. Quoted in Stacewicz, *Winter Soldiers,* p. 177.
86. Quoted in Stacewicz, *Winter Soldiers,* pp. 217–18.
87. Quoted in Dougan and Lipsman, *A Nation Divided,* p. 178.
88. Quoted in Stacewicz, *Winter Soldiers,* pp. 243–44.
89. Quoted in Stacewicz, *Winter Soldiers,* p. 248.
90. Quoted in Dougan and Lipsman, *A Nation Divided,* p. 178.
91. Dougan and Lipsman, *A Nation Divided,* p. 178–79.
92. Quoted in Stacewicz, *Winter Soldiers,* p. 405.
93. Quoted in Zaroulis and Sullivan, *Who Spoke Up?* p. 367.

94. Hayden, *Reunion,* pp. 438–39.

95. Quoted in Zaroulis and Sullivan, *Who Spoke Up?* p. 371.

96. Quoted in Zaroulis and Sullivan, *Who Spoke Up?* p. 382.

97. Dougan and Lipsman, *A Nation Divided,* p. 179.

98. Ron Kovic, *Born on the Fourth of July.* New York: McGraw-Hill, 1976, pp. 168–69.

99. Jerry Rubin, *Growin Up at 37.* New York: M. Evans, 1976, pp. 90–91.

Epilogue: A War for America's Soul

100. Anderson, *The Movement and the Sixties,* p. 418.

101. Todd Gitlin, *Twilight of Common Dreams.* New York: Metropolitian Books, 1995, p. 68.

102. Gitlin, *Twilight of Common Dreams,* p. 72.

103. McNamara, *In Retrospect,* p. 322.

✫ For Further Reading ✫

Terry H. Anderson, *The Movement and the Sixties*. New York: Oxford University Press, 1995. A book that details the historic social movements of the 1960s, from civil rights sit-ins to the antiwar marches to the women's liberation movement. Also explores the struggle for equality for African Americans, Native Americans, women, Chicanos, and others.

Joan Baez, *And a Voice to Sing With*. New York: New American Library, 1987. The memoir of the singer known as the Queen of Folk, whose passion for equal rights and nonviolence placed her at the center of dozens of civil rights marches and antiwar rallies.

Stewart Burns, *Social Movements of the 1960s*. Boston: Twayne, 1990. This volume of the "Social Movements" series covers the rise of the antiwar, civil rights, and women's liberation movements, and their long-ranging influences on Western society and culture.

Ronald Chepesiuk, *Sixties Radicals, Then and Now: Candid Conversations with Those Who Shaped the Era*. Jefferson, NC: McFarland, 1995. Interviews with '60s activists such as Dave Dellinger, Jerry Rubin, Abbie and Anita Hoffman, and fifteen others who helped shape the public antiwar effort; provides an interesting perspective of radicals looking back from the '90s.

Clark Dougan and Samuel Lipsman, eds., *A Nation Divided*. Boston: Boston Publishing, 1984. One of the books in "The Vietnam Experience" series, this edition explores events in the United States during the time of the Vietnam War, including the protest movement, those who opposed the protesters, and media perspectives.

Abbie Hoffman, *The Best of Abbie Hoffman*. New York: Four Walls Eight Windows, 1989. A compilation of Yippie! co-founder Abbie Hoffman's best writing over the years, including excerpts from his groundbreaking books *Revolution for the Hell of It, Woodstock Nation,* and *Steal This Book*. Also includes newer articles written in the 1980s.

Ron Kovic, *Born on the Fourth of July*. New York: McGraw-Hill, 1976. After being shot in the spine in Vietnam at the age of nineteen, Kovic was paralyzed from the chest down. He began to speak out against war in 1970. Film director Oliver Stone turned Kovic's book into a movie starring Tom Cruise in 1991.

Jerry Rubin, *Do It!* New York: Ballantine

Books, 1970. One of the most radical books of the '60s, written by one of the founders of the Yippies! who tells students to drop out, resist authority, and foment revolution against schools, government, corporations, and society. *Do It!* traces Rubin's life from a straight-laced sports reporter to a revolutionary agitator against the Vietnam War in the late '60s.

Jane and Michael Stern, *Sixties People.* New York: Alfred A. Knopf, 1990. An amusing book about the mods, hippies, hipsters, surfers, bikers, and other characters who populated '60s fads and fashion.

Time-Life Books, *Turbulent Years: The 60s.* Alexandria, VA: Time-Life Books, 1998. A big, colorful volume that covers all aspects of 1960s culture, including the war in Vietnam, assassinations, hippies, communes, rock and roll, and the antiwar movement.

★ Works Consulted ★

Edward Doyle and Samuel Lipsman, eds., *Setting the Stage*. Boston: Boston Publishing, 1981. Another in "The Vietnam Experience" series, this one focuses on the culture of Vietnam from ancient times until the prewar years, including the many wars and conflicts that have occurred in Vietnam over the centuries.

James William Gibson, "Revisiting Vietnam, Again," *Harper's Magazine*, April 2000. A review of the book *American Tragedy: Kennedy, Johnson, and the Origins of the Vietnam War*, by David Kaiser, who argues that Kennedy might have quickly ended the Vietnam War had he not been assassinated in 1963.

Todd Gitlin, *The Sixties: Years of Hope, Days of Rage*. New York: Bantam Books, 1987. The author, a respected professor of sociology at UC Berkeley, writes an in-depth study of a decade that he helped shape as a president of SDS and an organizer of the nation's first antiwar march.

———, *Twilight of Common Dreams*. New York: Metropolitan Books, 1995. The author looks at the 1990s from the perspective of the 1960s and explores the causes for the great cultural wars that have come to divide America since Vietnam.

David Lance Goines, *The Free Speech Movement: Coming of Age in the 1960s*. Berkeley, CA: Ten Speed Press, 1993. Studies the social and cultural aspects of the Berkeley Free Speech Movement, which quickly transformed into the antiwar movement.

David Harris, *Our War: What We Did in Vietnam and What It Did to Us*. New York: Times Books, 1996. Harris was married to folksinger Joan Baez, which made him one of the more famous draft resisters of the '60s. In the movie *Woodstock* Baez dedicates a song to Harris, who at the time was serving two years in a federal prison for refusing to register for the draft.

Tom Hayden, *Reunion: A Memoir*. New York: Random House, 1988. An autobiography by a man who was one of the founding members of the SDS, led dozens of protests in the '60s, and was put on trial for conspiracy after the Chicago Democratic convention. Hayden later went on to marry actress Jane Fonda and served many years as a state assemblyman in California.

Abbie Hoffman, *Soon to Be a Major Motion Picture*. New York: Perigee Books, 1980. The autobiography of Abbie Hoffman detailing his childhood in Massachusetts and his elevation to a national leader as one of the founders of the Yippies!.

Charles Kaiser, *1968 in America.* New York: Weidenfeld & Nicolson, 1988. A book about the startling events that took place during one single year that changed the country forever. That year saw President Johnson refuse to seek a second term because of the losses in Vietnam, the assassinations of Senator Robert Kennedy and Martin Luther King Jr., widespread rioting in urban neighborhoods, and bloody protests in Chicago.

Peter B. Levy, ed., *America in the Sixties: Right, Left, and Center.* Westport, CT: Praeger, 1998. This book tells the history of the 1960s in documents, articles, and journalism from that era, including the Gulf of Tonkin Resolution, Martin Luther King's "Letter from a Birmingham City Jail," and other historic writings.

Robert S. McNamara, *In Retrospect: The Tragedy and Lessons of Vietnam.* New York: Random House, 1995. The author, secretary of defense under Kennedy and Johnson during the Vietnam War, uses hundreds of formerly top-secret, classified documents and draws on his experience to arrive at the conclusion that the war was a tragic mistake.

James Miller, *"Democracy in the Streets": From Port Huron to the Siege of Chicago.* New York: Simon and Schuster, 1987. This book focuses on the politics, philosophies, and personalities of the 1960s protest movements, from the peaceful statements of the SDS in the early '60s to the violent street clashes with police at the 1968 Democratic convention in Chicago.

Joan Morrison and Robert K. Morrison, eds., *From Camelot to Kent State: The Sixties Experience in the Words of Those Who Lived It.* New York: Times Books, 1987. This book details the lives of fifty-nine men and women who lived through the social, political, and cultural turmoil of the 1960s.

Thomas Powers, *The War at Home.* New York: Grossman, 1973. A history of the opposition to the war in Vietnam written immediately after the United States ended its involvement in Southeast Asia. The author is a Pulitzer Prize–winning reporter who explores the methods of the ragtag group of disorganized activists who "brought the war home" and made headlines throughout the 1960s and early '70s.

Jerry Rubin, *Growing Up at 37.* New York: M. Evans, 1976. After the 1960s revolution, Yippie! cofounder Rubin set about to make changes in his personal life, as opposed to changing politics. This book details Rubin's story of personal growth and maturity as he looks back on his youthful revolt during the war.

Richard Stacewicz, *Winter Soldiers: An Oral History of Vietnam Veterans Against the War.* New York: Twayne, 1997. The author brings together more than thirty Vietnam veterans who later joined the Vietnam Veterans Against the War. The book poignantly records the words of the vets as they discuss Vietnam and their experiences after they were discharged and became leaders in the antiwar movement.

Irwin Unger and Debi Unger, eds., *The Times Were a Changin': The Sixties Reader.* New York: Three Rivers Press, 1998. An anthology of speeches, manifestos, and journalism of the 1960s, including essays on the Columbia uprising, speeches from Martin Luther King Jr., and official press releases from antiwar movement organizers.

Elaine Woo, "Lottery Rolled the Dice of Life for Draft-Age Men," *Los Angeles Times,* April 22, 2000. One of an informative series of articles that appeared in the *Times* about the cultural and historical legacy of the war in Vietnam both at home and abroad. The article was part of the "Lessons and Legacies" series that was written to commemorate the twenty-fifth anniversary of the fall of Saigon to Communist forces.

Nancy Zaroulis and Gerald Sullivan, *Who Spoke Up? American Protest Against the War in Vietnam 1963–1975.* Garden City, NY: Doubleday, 1984. A year-by-year record of the actions of those who spoke out against the Vietnam War, along with the triumphs and failures of the antiwar movement.

☆ Index ☆

★ Picture Credits ★

Cover photo: © Ted Streshinsky/Corbis
Agence France Presse/Archive Photos, 89
Archive Photos, 11 (both), 22, 30, 31, 37, 43, 47, 55 (both), 68, 93, 95
© AFP/Corbis, 67
© Bettmann/Corbis, 9, 13, 14, 17, 19, 44, 50, 58, 60, 63, 64, 71, 74, 76, 77, 78, 81, 83, 87
CNP/Archive Photos, 16
Andrew DeLory/Archive Photos, 24
Express Newspapers/K878/Archive Photos, 15
FPG International, 26, 34, 41, 86
Bernard Gotfryd/Archive Photos, 35
© Hulton-Deutsch Collection/Corbis, 28
Library of Congress, 45, 51, 53
© Guy Motil/Corbis, 39
National Archives, 32, 48
© Reuters NewMedia Inc./Corbis, 92, 96
William L. Rukeyser/Archive Photos, 66
Martha Schierholz, 10
© Ted Streshinsky/Corbis, 7

⋆ About the Author ⋆

Stuart A. Kallen is the author of more than 150 nonfiction books for children and young adults. He has written on topics ranging from the theory of relativity to rock and roll history to life on the American frontier. In addition, Mr. Kallen has written award-winning children's videos and television scripts. In his spare time, Stuart A. Kallen is a singer/songwriter/guitarist in San Diego, California.